daybook, *n.* a book in which the events of the day are recorded; *specif.* a journal or diary

TEACHER'S GUIDE

DAYBOOK
. . . .
of Critical Reading and Writing

GRADE 12

FRAN CLAGGETT

LOUANN REID

RUTH VINZ

Great Source Education Group
a Houghton Mifflin Company
Wilmington, Massachusetts

www.greatsource.com

A u t h o r s

Fran Claggett, currently an educational consultant for schools throughout the country and teacher at Sonoma State University, taught high school English for more than thirty years. She is author of several books, including *Drawing Your Own Conclusions: Graphic Strategies for Reading, Writing, and Thinking* (1992) and *A Measure of Success* (1996).

Louann Reid taught junior and senior high school English, speech, and drama for nineteen years and currently teaches courses for future English teachers at Colorado State University. Author of numerous articles and chapters, her first books were *Learning the Landscape* and *Recasting the Text* with Fran Claggett and Ruth Vinz (1996).

Ruth Vinz, currently a professor and director of English education at Teachers College, Columbia University, taught in secondary schools for twenty-three years. She is author of several books and numerous articles that discuss teaching and learning in the English classroom as well as a frequent presenter, consultant, and co-teacher in schools throughout the country.

Printed in the United States of America

International Standard Book Number: 0-669-46439-2

1 2 3 4 5 6 7 8 9 10 — POO — 04 03 02 01 00 99 98

Great Source wishes to acknowledge the many insights and improvements made to the *Daybooks* thanks to the work of the following teachers and educators.

Readers

Jay Amberg
Glenbrook South High School
Glenview, Illinois

Joanne Arellanes
Rancho Cordova, California

Nancy Bass
Moore Middle School
Arvada, Colorado

Jim Benny
Sierra Mountain Middle School
Truckee, California

Noreen Benton
Guilderland High School
Altamont, New York

Janet Bertucci
Hawthorne Junior High School
Vernon Hills, Illinois

Jim Burke
Burlingame High School
Burlingame, California

Mary Castellano
Hawthorne Junior High School
Vernon Hills, Illinois

Diego Davalos
Chula Vista High School
Chula Vista, California

Jane Detgen
Daniel Wright Middle School
Lake Forest, Illinois

Michelle Ditzian
Shepard Junior High School
Deerfield, Illinois

Jenni Dunlap
Highland Middle School
Libertyville, Illinois

Judy Elman
Highland Park High School
Highland Park, Illinois

Mary Ann Evans-Patrick
Fox Valley Writing Project
Oshkosh, Wisconsin

Howard Frishman
Twin Grove Junior High School
Buffalo Grove, Illinois

Kathleen Gaynor
Wheaton, Illinois

Beatrice Gerrish
Bell Middle School
Golden, Colorado

Kathy Glass
San Carlos, California

Alton Greenfield
Minnesota Dept. of Child,
Family & Learning
St. Paul, Minnesota

Sue Hebson
Deerfield High School
Deerfield, Illinois

Carol Jago
Santa Monica High School
Santa Monica, California

Diane Kepner
Oakland, California

Lynne Ludwig
Gregory Middle School
Naperville, Illinois

Joan Markos-Horejs
Fox Valley Writing Project
Oshkosh, Wisconsin

James McDermott
South High Community School
Worcester, Massachusetts

Tim McGee
Worland High School
Worland, Wyoming

Mary Jane Mulholland
Lynn Classical High School
Lynn, Massachusetts

Lisa Myers
Englewood, Colorado

Karen Neilsen
Desert Foothills Middle School
Phoenix, Arizona

Jayne Allen Nichols
El Camino High School
Sacramento, California

Mary Nicolini
Penn Harris High School
Mishawaka, Indiana

Lucretia Pannozzo
John Jay Middle School
Katonah, New York

Robert Pavlick
Marquette University
Milwaukee, Wisconsin

Linda Popp
Gregory Middle School
Naperville, Illinois

Caroline Ratliffe
Fort Bend Instructional School District
Sugar Land, Texas

Guerrino Rich
Akron North High School
Akron, Ohio

Shirley Rosson
Alief Instructional School District
Houston, Texas

Alan Ruter
Glenbrook South High School
Glenview, Illinois

Rene Schillenger
Washington, D.C.

Georgianne Schulte
Oak Park Middle School
Oak Park, Illinois

Carol Schultz
Tinley Park, Illinois

Wendell Schwartz
Adlai E. Stevenson High School
Lincolnshire, Illinois

Lynn Snell
Oak Grove School
Green Oaks, Illinois

Hildi Spritzer
Oakland, California

Bill Stone
Plano Senior High School
Plano, Texas

Barbara Thompson
Hazelwood School
Florissant, Missouri

Elma Torres
Orange Grove Instructional
School District
Orange Grove, Texas

Bill Weber
Libertyville High School
Libertyville, Illinois

Darby Williams
Sacramento, California

Hillary Zunin
Napa High School
Napa, California

Table of Contents

O v e r v i e w

What is a daybook and what is it good for? These are the first questions asked about this series, *Daybooks of Critical Reading and Writing*.

The answer is that a daybook is a keepable, journal-like book that helps improve students' reading and writing. *Daybooks* are a tool to promote daily reading and writing in classrooms. By immersing students in good literature and by asking them to respond creatively to it, the *Daybooks* combine critical reading and creative, personal response to literature.

The literature in each *Daybook* has been chosen to complement the selections commonly found in anthologies and the most commonly taught novels. Most of the literature selections are brief and designed to draw students into them by their brevity and high-interest appeal. In addition, each passage has a literary quality that will be probed in the lesson.

Each lesson focuses on a specific aspect of critical reading—that is, the reading skills used by good readers. These aspects of critical reading are summarized in closing statements positioned at the end of each lesson. To organize this wide-ranging analysis into critical reading, the authors have constructed a framework called the "Angles of Literacy."

This framework organizes the lessons and units in the *Daybook*. The five Angles of Literacy described here are:

- marking or annotating the text
- examining the story connections
- looking at a text from multiple perspectives
- studying the language and craft of a text
- focusing on individual authors

The Angles of Literacy are introduced in the first cluster of the *Daybook* and then explored in greater depth in subsequent clusters.

The *Daybook* concept was developed to help teachers with a number of practical concerns:

1. To introduce daily (or at least weekly) critical reading and writing into classrooms

2. To fit into the new configurations offered by block scheduling

3. To create a literature book students can own, allowing them to mark up the literature and write as they read

4. To make an affordable literature book that students can carry home

How to Use the Daybook

As the *Daybooks* were being developed, more than fifty teachers commented on and reviewed the lesson concept and individual lessons and units. From their comments several main uses for the *Daybooks* emerged.

1. BLOCK SCHEDULING

Daybook activities were designed to accommodate block-scheduled class periods. With longer periods, teachers commented on the need to introduce two to four parts to each "block," one of which would be a *Daybook* lesson. The brief, self-contained lessons fit perfectly at the beginning or end of a block and could be used to complement or build upon another segment of the day.

2. ELECTIVES

With the advent of block scheduling, more electives are being added to the curriculum. Course slots now exist once again for poetry, reading for college, creative writing, and contemporary writers. Teachers found a number of different course slots in which to use the *Daybooks*, mostly because of the strong combination of literature, critical reading, and creative writing.

3. CORE READING LIST

For high schools guided by a list of core readings, the *Daybooks* offered a convenient way to add some daily writing and critical reading instruction to classes. Plus, the emphasis on newer, contemporary writers seemed to these teachers to open up the traditional curriculum with new voices.

4. SUPPLEMENTING AN ANTHOLOGY

For literature teachers using older anthologies, the *Daybook* offers an easy, economical means of updating their literature curriculums. The multitude of newer, contemporary authors and wide range of multicultural authors added nicely to literature classes.

The reviewers of the *Daybooks* proved that no two classrooms are alike. While each was unique in its own way, every teacher found uses for the *Daybook* lessons in the classroom. In the end, the usefulness of the *Daybooks* derived from the blend of elements they offer:

- direct instruction on how to read critically
- regular and explicit practice in marking up and annotating texts
- "writing to learn" activities for each day or week
- great selections from contemporary (and often multicultural) literature
- in-depth instruction in how to read literature and write effectively about it

Organization of the Daybooks

Each *Daybook* has 16 units, or clusters, of five lessons. The 80 lessons afford daily work over a single semester or work two or three times each week for an entire year. A lesson is designed to last approximately 30 minutes, although some lessons will surely extend longer, depending on how energetically students attack the writing activities. But the intent throughout was to create brief, potent lessons that integrate quality literature, critical reading instruction, and writing.

The unifying concept behind these lessons is the Angles of Literacy—the idea that a selection can be approached from at least five directions:

- by annotating and marking up the text
- by analyzing the story connections in the literature
- by examining the text from different perspectives
- by studying the language and craft of the writer
- by focusing closely on all of the aspects of a single writer's work

A lesson typically begins with an introduction and leads quickly into a literary selection. Occasionally the purpose is to direct students' attention to a specific aspect of the selection; but just as often students are asked to read and formulate a response on their own. By looking closely at the selection, students are able to discover what can be learned through careful reading. Students are led to look again at the selection and to respond analytically, reflectively, and creatively to what they have read.

boldface terms in glossary

...ight. (William Shakespeare, So...
assonance and consonance.)

allusion, a reference in a literary work to a familiar person, place or thing.

annotation, a note or comment added to a text ...ction, explain, or critique the text...

unit title

focus on critical reading

lesson title

initial response activity

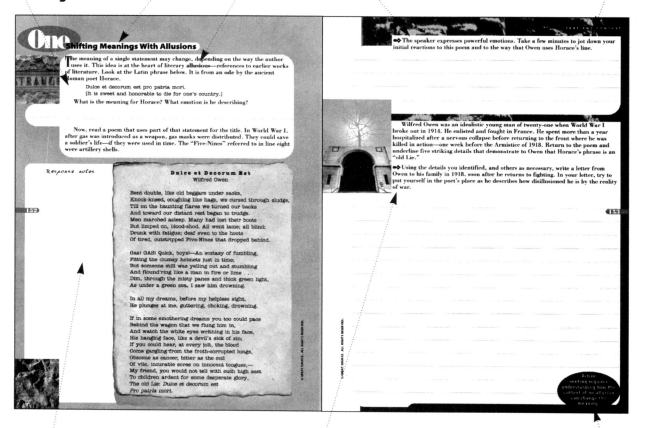

One

Shifting Meanings With Allusions

The meaning of a single statement may change, depending on the way the author uses it. This idea is at the heart of literary allusions—references to earlier works of literature. Look at the Latin phrase below. It is from an ode by the ancient Roman poet Horace.

Dulce et decorum est pro patria mori.
[It is sweet and honorable to die for one's country.]

What is the meaning for Horace? What emotion is he describing?

Now, read a poem that uses part of that statement for the title. In World War I, after gas was introduced as a weapon, gas masks were distributed. They could save a soldier's life—if they were used in time. The "Five-Nines" referred to in line eight were artillery shells.

Response notes

132

Dulce et Decorum Est
Wilfred Owen

Bent double, like old beggars under sacks,
Knock-kneed, coughing like hags, we cursed through sludge,
Till on the haunting flares we turned our backs
And toward our distant rest began to trudge.
Men marched asleep. Many had lost their boots
But limped on, blood-shod. All went lame; all blind;
Drunk with fatigue; deaf even to the hoots
Of tired, outstripped Five-Nines that dropped behind.

Gas! GAS! Quick, boys!—An ecstasy of fumbling,
Fitting the clumsy helmets just in time;
But someone still was yelling out and stumbling
And flound'ring like a man in fire or lime . . .
Dim, through the misty panes and thick green light,
As under a green sea, I saw him drowning.

In all my dreams, before my helpless sight,
He plunges at me, guttering, choking, drowning.

If in some smothering dreams you too could pace
Behind the wagon that we flung him in,
And watch the white eyes writhing in his face,
His hanging face, like a devil's sick of sin;
If you could hear, at every jolt, the blood
Come gargling from the froth-corrupted lungs,
Obscene as cancer, bitter as the cud
Of vile, incurable sores on innocent tongues,—
My friend, you would not tell with such high zest
To children ardent for some desperate glory,
The old Lie: Dulce et decorum est
Pro patria mori.

➥ The speaker expresses powerful emotions. Take a few minutes to jot down your initial reactions to this poem and to the way that Owen uses Horace's line.

Wilfred Owen was an idealistic young man of twenty-one when World War I broke out in 1914. He enlisted and fought in France. He spent more than a year hospitalized after a nervous collapse before returning to the front where he was killed in action—one week before the Armistice of 1918. Return to the poem and underline five striking details that demonstrate to Owen that Horace's phrase is an "old Lie."

➥ Using the details you identified, and others as necessary, write a letter from Owen to his family in 1918, soon after he returns to fighting. In your letter, try to put yourself in the poet's place as he describes how disillusioned he is by the reality of war.

133

Active reading requires understanding how the context of an allusion can change the meaning.

space for annotations

longer, interpretive response to literature

summary statement

Frequently Asked Questions

One benefit of the extensive field-testing of the *Daybooks* was to highlight right at the beginning several questions about the *Daybooks*.

1. WHAT IS A DAYBOOK ANYWAY?

A daybook used to be "a book in which daily transactions are recorded" or "a diary." Most recently, the word has been used to mean "journal." To emphasize the daily reading and writing, the authors chose the word *daybook* rather than *journal*. And, indeed, the *Daybooks* are much more than journals, in that they include literature selections and instruction in critical reading.

2. ARE STUDENTS SUPPOSED TO WRITE IN THE *DAYBOOK*?

Yes, definitely. Only by physically marking the text will students become active readers. To interact with a text and take notes as an active reader, students must write in their *Daybooks*. Students will have a written record of their thoughts, questions, brainstorms, annotations, and creative responses. The immediacy of reading and responding on the page is an integral feature of the *Daybooks*. Students will also benefit from the notebook-like aspect, allowing them to double back to earlier work, see progress, store ideas, and record responses. The *Daybook* serves, in a way, like a portfolio. It is one simple form of portfolio assessment.

3. CAN I PHOTOCOPY THESE LESSONS?

No, unfortunately, you cannot. The selections, instruction, and activities are protected by copyright. To copy them infringes on the rights of the authors of the selections and the book. Writers such as Octavio Paz, Toni Morrison, and Ray Bradbury have granted permission for the use of their work in the *Daybook*, and to photocopy their work violates their copyright.

4. CAN I SKIP AROUND IN THE *DAYBOOK*?

Yes, absolutely. The *Daybooks* were designed to allow teachers maximum flexibility. You can start with some of the later clusters (or units) and then pick up the earlier ones later on in the year. Or you can teach a lesson from here and one from there. But the optimum order of the book is laid out in the table of contents, and students will most likely see the logic and continuity of the book when they start at the beginning and proceed in order.

5. WHAT IS "ANNOTATING A TEXT"? ARE STUDENTS SUPPOSED TO WRITE IN THE MARGIN OF THE BOOK?

Annotating refers to underlining parts of a text, circling words or phrases, highlighting with a colored marker, or taking notes in the margin. Students begin their school years marking up books in kindergarten and end, often in college, writing in the margins of their texts or highlighting key passages. Yet in the years in between—the majority of their school years—students are often forbidden from writing in their books, even though it represents a natural kinesthetic aid for memory and learning.

6. WHY WERE THESE LITERATURE SELECTIONS CHOSEN?

The *Daybooks* are intended to complement high school classrooms, most of which use literature anthologies or have core lists of novels that they teach. In either instance, the literature taught tends to be traditional. Adding contemporary selections is the best way to complement existing curriculums.

The literature was also chosen to illustrate the lesson idea. (A lesson on story characters, for example, needed to present two or three strong characters for study.) So, in addition to being chosen for appeal for students, selections illustrate the specific aspect of critical reading focused on in that lesson.

7. WHAT ARE THE ART AND PHOTOS SUPPOSED TO REPRESENT?

The art program for the *Daybooks* features the work of outstanding contemporary photographers. These photos open each unit and set the tone. Then, within each lesson, a number of smaller, somewhat enigmatic images are used. The purpose behind these images is not to illustrate what is happening in the literature or even to represent an interpretation of it. Rather, the hope is to stretch students' minds, hinting at connections, provoking the imagination, jarring loose a random thought or two about the selection. And, of course, the hope is that students will respond favorably to contemporary expressions of creativity.

8. WHAT ARE THE BOLDFACE TERMS IN THE LESSON ALL ABOUT?

The terms boldfaced in the lessons appear in a glossary in the back of the *Daybook*. The glossary includes key literary terms
    1) that are used in the *Daybook* lessons and
    2) that students are likely to encounter in literature classes.

The glossary is another resource for students to use in reading and reacting to the literature.

Correlation to Writers INC

Like the *Writers INC* handbook, the *Daybooks* will appeal to certain teachers who need versatile, flexible materials and who place a premium on books with high student appeal. Some teachers, by nature, are more eclectic in their teaching approach: others more consistent and patterned. Some teachers place a premium on student interest and relevance more than on structured, predictable lessons. The *Daybooks*, like *Writers INC*, are directed at more eclectic teachers and classrooms.

The *Daybooks* are organized to allow maximum flexibility. You can pick an individual lesson or cluster of lessons in order to feature a certain author or literary selection. Or, you may want to concentrate on a particular area of critical reading. In either case, the *Daybooks*, like *Writers INC*, allow you to pick up the book and use it for days or weeks at a time, then leave it, perhaps to teach a novel or longer writing project, and then return to it again later in the semester. You, not the text, set the classroom agenda.

Another great similarity between the *Daybooks* and the *Writers INC* handbook lies in the approach to writing. Both begin from the premise that writing is, first and foremost, a means of discovery. "Writing to learn" is the common expression for this idea. Only by expression can we discover what lies within us. *Writers INC* introduces this idea in its opening chapter, and the *Daybooks*, by promoting daily writing, give you the tool to make writing a consistent, regular feature of your classes.

But the *Daybooks* only start students on a daily course of reading and writing. Individual writing assignments are initiated but not carried through to final drafts. The purpose of writing in the *Daybooks* is mostly one of discovery, creative expression, clarification of ideas or interpretations, and idea generation. The *Daybooks* are intended to be starting points, places to ruminate and organize thoughts about literature, as opposed to offering definitive instructions about how to craft an essay or write a persuasive letter. That's where *Writers INC* comes in. It picks up where the *Daybooks* leave off, providing everything students need to create a polished essay or literary work.

The accompanying chart correlates writing assignments in the *Daybooks* to *Writers INC*.

Daybook Lesson	Writing Activity	*Writers INC* reference
Angles of Literacy		
1. Interacting With a Text	write a paragraph	103-104, 444
2. Story Connections	describe a personal experience	21, 111, 286-288, 444
3. Shifting Perspectives	react to a poem	339, 423, 444, 554
4. Language and Craft	examine a poem's imagery	354-355, 421, 444
5. Focus on the Writer	design a book cover	444, 555

Daybook Lesson	Writing Activity	Writers INC reference
Building an Interpretation		
1. Subject and Story Meaning	answer questions	400, 418
2. Conflict and Story Meaning	complete a chart	400, 418
3. Conveying Meaning Through Tone	rewrite a description	425, 554
4. Imagery and Meaning	analyze imagery	354-355, 400, 412
5. Interpreting Meaning	write an essay	116-117, 121, 356
Literary Belief		
1. How Readers Come to Believe	write a paragraph	103-110
2. Creating Believability	react to a story's ending	120, 400
3. Writing Unwritten Scenes	write a scene	64, 319, 555
4. Believing the Fantastic	explain a passage	120, 400, 412
5. Creating a Believable Fantasy	write a fantasy story	21, 311-312, 319
Seeing the World		
1. Considering Sources	analyze author's attitude	398-400, 412
2. Identifying Inner Conflict	describe author's conflicts	398-400, 418, 494
3. Real and Imaginary Details	complete a chart	398-400, 494
4. Point of View	analyze author's purpose	120, 412, 424
5. Establishing Points of Reference	analyze details	120, 398-400, 412
Perspectives on a Subject: Finding a Home		
1. Idea Association	write a description	75, 111, 137
2. Defining a Subject Through Objects	react to descriptive details	339, 398-400
3. Developing Contrasts	describe a place	64, 111, 137
4. Changing Perspectives	continue a poem	313, 444
5. Irony and Double Meanings	write a description	64, 111, 137, 286

Daybook Lesson	Writing Activity	Writers INC reference
Writing from Models		
1. Point of View	write a poem	311-313, 444
2. Spinoff Modeling	write a poem	311-313, 444
3. Modeling an Ode	compose an ode	311-313, 316-317, 444
4. Modeling Voice	write an emulation	311-313, 440, 444
5. Modeling Situation	write a poem	311-313, 444
Crafting Memory		
1. Images of Childhood	analyze a poem's imagery	354-356, 412, 444
2. Childhood Memory	write a poem	111, 313, 444
3. The Language of Memory	write a personal narrative	21, 111, 445
4. Stream of Consciousness	describe a character	304, 445
5. Daydreaming and Epiphanies	describe a personal experience	64, 111, 445
William Butler Yeats		
1. Image and Symbol	analyze symbolism	354-356, 412, 444
2. The Dramatic Lyric	analyze imagery	412, 421, 444
3. Lines That Transcend Time	react to a poem	339, 400, 444
4. Poem as Autobiography	write a poem	75, 313, 444
5. The Artistic Process	react to author's statement	339, 400, 494, 560
Essentials of Reading		
1. Thinking With the Writer	make and analyze predictions	412, 496
2. Reading Between the Lines	complete a chart	120, 412
3. Thinking Theme	summarize a story's theme	425, 497, 499
4. Doubling Back	reflect on a character	339, 400
5. Author's Purpose	rewrite a story	496, 499

Daybook Lesson	Writing Activity	Writers INC reference
Experiencing the Story		
1. Tension and Anticipation	describe a personal experience	21, 287
2. Empathy and Sympathy	continue a story	319, 445
3. Observer and Participant	reflect on a story	111, 339, 412
4. Then and Now	write a paragraph	103-110, 554
5. Creating the Experience	write a personal narrative	21, 64, 111, 287
Language and Story		
1. Word Play	describe a poem's situation	400, 418, 444
2. Language and Tone	write a story	319, 554-555
3. Reading Difficult Language	translate a poem's language	75, 440, 498
4. Language and Characterization	analyze characters	356, 398-400, 412
5. Creating Meaning Through Language	draft a story	21, 319, 554
Text and Context		
1. Shifting Meanings With Allusions	write a letter	444, 497, 554
2. The Context of Geography	write a paragraph	103-110, 444
3. Shifting Personal Perspectives	write from a child's perspective	111, 554-555
4. The Context of Politics	explain an essay's conclusion	339, 412, 494
5. The Events of History	write a poem	313, 444
Interpreting Nonfiction		
1. The Perspective of the Author	examine author's perspective	339, 398-400
2. Aspects of the Subject	create a web	298, 554
3. Understanding an Opinion	discuss meaning	339, 494
4. Reading an Argumentative Essay	write an argument	120, 339, 398-400
5. Understanding Arguments	write a description	111, 349-352

Daybook Lesson	Writing Activity	*Writers INC* reference
Character in Poetry		
1. Understanding Character	compose comparisons	65, 444, 554
2. The Dramatic Monologue	write a character sketch	304, 444
3. Reading a Long Poem	analyze a poem	410, 412, 444
4. Direct Address	explain a line of poetry	410, 412, 444, 498
5. Completing the Reading	explain a poem's meaning	410, 412, 444
Poetry and Art		
1. The Art of Irony	explain irony	412, 421, 444, 538
2. Visualizing a Poem	create a scene	64, 444, 496
3. Discovering Possible Interpretations	interpret a poem	120, 444
4. Comparing Poems	compare two poems	434, 444, 549
5. Exploration and Interpretation	reflect on a poem	339, 400, 444
V. S. Naipaul		
1. Creating Characters	write a character sketch	304, 398-400, 445
2. Replaying the Newsreel	examine imagery	410, 412, 421
3. Finding a Place in the World	agree or disagree with a statement	339, 365, 400, 560
4. The Writer in the World	write a personal narrative	21, 111, 287
5. A Portrait of the Writer	write about an author	339, 559-560

Angles of Literacy

by Louann Reid

When we view something of potential value, such as a diamond or an antique vase, we often examine it from all sides. We hold it up and slowly turn it, looking first at the front, then the sides and back. Combining information from each perspective, we construct a fuller picture of the object and its worth.

Similarly, we can examine a concept or an idea from several angles, or perspectives, using a variety of approaches to understand a complex concept. Perhaps no concept in education is more complex—or more important—than literacy.

"Literacy" is frequently defined as the ability to read and write. But people also need to be able to read critically, write effectively, draw diagrams, collaborate with others, listen carefully, and understand complex instructions. In short, literacy means being able to do whatever is required to communicate effectively in a variety of situations. Angles of Literacy is the term we use in these *Daybooks* to identify five approaches to becoming literate.

THE FIVE ANGLES

The Angles of Literacy are major perspectives from which to examine a text. Strategies within each angle further define each one. Activities in the *Daybooks* provide students with multiple opportunities to become autonomous users of the strategies on other literature that they will encounter.

The angles are listed in an order that reflects the way that readers and writers first engage with the text. They are encouraged to move gradually from that initial engagement to a more evaluative or critical stance where they study the author's language and craft, life and work. They critique the texts they read and consider what other critics have written. Moving from engagement through interpretation to evaluation is the process that Louise Rosenblatt and later reader-response critics advocate.

In our own work with secondary school students, we have repeatedly seen the value of encouraging students to read and write using all three stages— engagement, interpretation, evaluation. We also know that students sometimes begin at a different stage in the process—perhaps with interpretation rather than engagement. So, our five angles are not meant to be a hierarchy. Students may begin their engagement with the text using any angle and proceed in any order. Depending on the text and the context, readers might start with making personal connections to the stories in an essay. If the text is by an author that the students know well, they might naturally begin by comparing this work to the author's other works.

STRATEGIES

Strategies are plans or approaches to learning. By using some strategies over and over, students can learn to comprehend any text. The *Daybook* activities, such as annotating or visualizing a specific poem, story, or essay, provide students multiple opportunities to develop these strategies. From using this scaffolding students gradually become more independent readers and, ultimately, fully literate.

Because strategies are employed through activities, it may seem at first that they are the same thing. Yet, it is important to remember that a strategy is a purposeful plan. When, as readers, we select a strategy such as underlining key phrases, we have selected this action deliberately to help us differentiate between important information and unimportant information. We may use a double-entry log (an activity) to identify the metaphors in a poem. Our purpose in doing so is to understand figurative language (a strategy). Strategies are purposeful plans, often consisting of one or more activities, to help us comprehend and create.

At the end of each lesson, the strategies are explicitly stated. In a sentence or two, the main point of the activity is noted. When students complete all 80 lessons in a *Daybook*, they will have 80 statements of what they, as active readers, can do to read critically and write effectively.

Reflection is a vital component in helping students understand the use of strategies. After using a particular strategy, students need to step back and consider how the strategy worked or did not. They might think about how an approach or a strategy can change their understanding of what they read and write. Students might ask themselves a series of questions such as: What have I done? What have I learned? What would I do differently next time? How did the angle or strategy affect my understanding? What would I understand differently if I had changed the angle or the strategy?

ACTIVITIES

Each lesson in these *Daybooks* contains activities for students. From rereading to discussing with a partner to making a story chart, students learn how to become better critical readers and more effective writers. Many activities encourage students to write to learn. Other activities encourage students to increase their understanding of a text by visualizing it in a sketch or a graphic organizer. But, as much as possible, the *Daybooks* try to encourage students to make a creative written response with a poem, some dialogue, a character sketch, or some other creative assignment.

We have selected activities that work particularly well with the texts in the lesson and with the strategies we want students to develop. However, as you will see when you and your students use the *Daybooks*, there are several possible activities that could reinforce a particular strategy. You may want to have students try some of these activities, such as making a story chart or using a double-entry log, when they read other texts in class. This would also be another opportunity to have students ask themselves the reflective questions.

A n g l e s   o f   L i t e r a c y

ANGLE OF VISION	STRATEGIES	SELECTED ACTIVITIES
Interacting with a Text	• underlining key phrases • writing questions or comments in the margin • noting word patterns and repetitions • circling unknown words • keeping track of the story or idea as it unfolds	• Write down initial impressions. • Reread. • Write a summary of the poem. • Generate two questions and one "certainty." Then, discuss the questions and statement in a small group.
Making Connections to the Stories within a Text	• paying attention to the stories being told • connecting the stories to one's own experience • speculating on the meaning or significance of incidents	• Make a story chart with three columns—incident in the poem, significance of the incident, related incident in my life. • Write a news story of events behind the story in the poem.

Shifting Perspectives to Examine a Text from Many Points of View	• examining the point of view
	• changing the point of view
	• exploring various versions of an event
	• forming interpretations
	• comparing texts
	• asking "what if" questions
		• Discuss with a partner or small group how you might read a poem differently if:
		   the speaker were female
		   you believe the speaker is a parent
		• Rewrite the text from a different point of view.

Studying the Language and Craft of a Text	• understanding figurative language • looking at the way the author uses words • modeling the style of other writers • studying various kinds of literature	• Use a double-entry log to identify metaphors and the qualities implied by the comparison. • Examine the title of the poem and its relationship to the text.
Focusing on the Writer's Life and Work	• reading what the author says about the writing • reading what others say • making inferences about the connections between an author's life and work • analyzing the writer's style • paying attention to repeated themes and topics in the work by one author	• Read about the poet's life. Then make an inference chart to record evidence from the poet's life, an inference, and a comparison to the poem. • Write an evaluation of the poem. Then read what one or more critics have said about the poem or poet. Finally, write a short response, either agreeing or disagreeing with the critic. Support your ideas with textual evidence.

Responding to Literature Through Writing

by Ruth Vinz

We have found that students' encounters with literature are enriched when they write their way toward understanding. The writing activities in the *Daybooks* are intended to help students explore and organize their ideas and reactions during and after reading. We try to make use of the exploratory and clarifying roles of writing through various activities.

Exploratory assignments include those through which students question, analyze, annotate, connect, compare, personalize, emulate, map, or chart aspects in the literary selections. Generally these assignments aid students' developing interpretations and reactions to the subjects, themes, or literary devices in the literature they are reading. Other writing activities offer students the opportunity to clarify their understanding of what they've read. These assignments lead students to look at other perspectives, determine the significance of what they read, and prioritize, interpret, question, and reflect on initial impressions. Further, students are asked to create literature of their own as a way of applying the concepts they're learning. Writing to clarify also involves students in reflection, where they are asked to think about their reactions and working hypotheses. Taken together, the writing activities represent a series of strategies that students can apply to the complex task of reading literature.

The writing activities included in the *Daybooks* start students on the path toward understanding. We did not take it as the function of the writing activities in this book to lead students through the writing process toward final, finished drafts. Although examples of extensions are included here in the Teacher's Guide, the writing in the *Daybooks* introduces first draft assignments that may lead into more formal writing if you, as the teacher, so choose.

You will have your own ideas about assisting students with the writing activities or extending the writing beyond the *Daybooks*. We think it's important for you to remind students that the writing in which they engage is useful for their reading outside the *Daybooks*. For example, students may use various types of maps, charts, or diagrams introduced in the *Daybooks* when they read a novel. They may find that the response notes become a strategy they use regularly. Once exposed to imitation and modeling, students may find these useful tools for understanding an author's style, language, or structure. If your students develop a conscious awareness of the strategies behind the particular writing activities, they can apply these in other reading situations.

Writing assignments to explore and to clarify students' developing interpretations are incorporated in two types of activities, both of which are elaborated on below.

WRITING ABOUT LITERATURE

You will find activities in every cluster of lessons that call upon students to write about the literature they are reading. We developed these writing assignments to help facilitate, stimulate, support, and shape students' encounters with literature. We think the assignments have four purposes:

(1) to connect the literature to the students' personal experiences; (2) to re-examine the text for various purposes (language and craft, connections with other texts, shifting perspectives, developing interpretations); (3) to develop hypotheses, judgments, and critical interpretations; (4) to apply the idea behind the lesson to a new literary text or situation.

The types of writing we have used to fulfill these purposes are:

1. Response Notes

Students keep track of their initial responses to the literature by questioning, annotating, and marking up the text in various ways. The response notes are used to get students in the habit of recording what they are thinking while reading. Seldom do we begin by telling them what and how to write in this space. Many times we circle back and ask them to build on what they have written with a particular focus or way of responding. In the response notes, students are encouraged to make personal connections, re-examine text, jot down ideas for their own writing, and monitor their changing responses.

2. Personal Narrative

Students write personal stories that connect or relate to what they have read. In some cases, the narratives tell the stories of students' prior reading experiences or how a literary selection relates to their life experiences. Other activities use personal narrative to apply and refine students' understanding of narrative principles.

3. Idea Fund

Students collect ideas for writing—catalogs, lists, charts, clusters, diagrams, double-entry logs, sketches, or maps. These forms of idea gathering are useful for analyzing particular literary selections and will aid the initial preparation for longer pieces of critical analysis.

4. Short Response

Students write summaries; paraphrase main themes or ideas; and compose paragraphs of description, exposition, explanation, evaluation, and interpretation.

5. Analysis

Students write short analyses that take them beyond summarizing the literary selection or their personal reactions to it. The analytic activities engage students in recognizing symbols and figures of speech and the links between events, characters, or images. Again, these short analytical responses are intended to prepare students for longer, critical interpretation that you, as a teacher, might assign.

6. Speculation

Students' speculations are encouraged by writing activities that engage them in predicting, inferring, and imagining. "What if . . . ," "How might . . . ," and "Imagine that . . ." are all ways in which students are invited to see further possibilities in the literature they read.

Students use writing to record and reflect on their reactions and interpretations. At times, students are asked to share their writing with others. Such sharing is another form of reflection through which students have an opportunity to "see again" their own work in the context of what others have produced.

The writing activities in the *Daybooks* will help students connect what they read with what they experience and with what they write, and also to make connections between the literary selections and literary techniques. The activities encourage students to experiment with a range of forms, choose a range of focuses, and reflect on what they have learned from these. We hope the writing serves to give students access to a kind of literary experience they can value and apply in their future reading.

WRITING LITERATURE

Within a literary work, readers find a writer's vision, but readers also co-create the vision along with the writer and learn from his or her craft. We've asked our students to write literature of their own as a way of responding to what they read. Through writing literature, students can explore facets of the original work or use the techniques of a variety of authors. Here are a number of the activities introduced in the *Daybooks*:

1. Take the role of writer

Students write imaginative reconstructions of gaps in a text by adding another episode, adding dialogue, rewriting the ending, adding a section before or after the original text, adding characters, changing the setting, or creating dream sequences. Such imaginative entries into the text require that students apply their knowledge of the original.

2. Imitation and Modeling

The idea of modeling and imitation is not new. Writers learn from other writers. The modeling activities are intended to help students "read like a writer." In these activities, students experiment with nuances of expression, syntactic and other structural principles, and apply their knowledge of literary devices (for example, *rhythm, imagery, metaphor*). One goal in educating students with literature is to make explicit what writers do. One way to achieve the goal is to provide models that illustrate various principles of construction.

3. Original Pieces

Students write poems, character sketches, monologues, dialogues, episodes, vignettes, and descriptions as a way to apply the knowledge about language and craft they are gaining through their reading.

4. Living Others' Perspectives

Writing from others' points of view encourages students to step beyond self to imagine other perspectives. Students write from a character's point of view, compose diary entries or letters, explain others' positions or opinions, and other reactions to a situation. These writing activities encourage students to explore the concerns of others and to project other perspectives through their writing.

The writing becomes a record of students' developing and changing ideas about literature. By the time students have finished all of the writing in this book, they will have used writing strategies that can assist them in all future reading.

Reading, Writing, and Assessment

by Fran Claggett

As teachers, we all cope with the complexities of assessing student performance. We must be careful readers of student work, attentive observers of student participation in various activities, and focused writers in responding to student work. We must understand the value of rewarding what students do well and encouraging them to improve. Above all, we need to make the criteria for assessment clear to students.

THE DAYBOOKS

The *Daybooks* provide visible accounts of many aspects of the reading process. Students record all the various permutations of active reading and writing. In the current view of most teachers and researchers, reading is a process of constructing meaning through transactions with a text. In this view, the individual reader assumes responsibility for interpreting a text, guided not only by the language of the text but also by the associations, cultural experiences, and prior knowledge that the reader brings to the interpretive task. Meaning does not reside solely within the words on the page. Our view of reading emphasizes the role of the reader. Construction of meaning, rather than the gaining and displaying of knowledge, should be the goal of reading instruction. This rule is reflected throughout the *Daybooks*, which guide students in how to read, respond to, interpret, and reflect on carefully selected works of literature.

Within these lessons, students interact with a text from five angles of literacy. The *Daybooks* make it possible for both students and teachers to track students' increasing sophistication in using the angles to make sense of their reading. Through the strategies presented in the lessons, students learn to express their understanding of a text. They will do such things as show their understanding of figurative language and the importance of form; write about how characters are developed and change; and demonstrate their understanding of how a piece of literature develops.

THE ROLE OF THE TEACHER

The teacher is critical to the *Daybook* agenda. Conceivably, a teacher could pass out the *Daybooks* and turn the students loose, but that would not result in the carefully guided reading and writing that is intended. Rather, the teachers are central to student success. Because of the format of the *Daybooks*, lessons are short, each taking no more than a normal class period. They are intended to be complete in themselves, yet most teachers will see that there are numerous opportunities for extensions, elaborations, further readings, group work, and writing. The Teacher's Guide provides some suggestions; you will think of many others. The *Daybooks* offer guidelines for reading and thinking, for writing and drawing used in the service of reading. They also provide many opportunities for students to write pieces of their own, modeling, responding, interpreting, and reflecting on the pieces that they have read. Many of these pieces might lead to later revision, refining, group response, and editing. It is the teacher, however, who knows the students well enough to see which pieces would be worthwhile to work with and which it is best to leave as exercises rather than completed works.

In assessing the *Daybooks*, it is important to remember to look at the students' growing facility with the processes of reading. As is true with all learning, there will be false starts, abandoned practices, and frustrations, yet also illuminations, progress, and occasional epiphanies. No music teacher ever graded every attempt at mastering a piece of music. We, too, must resist the urge—honed by years of assessing only products or finished papers—of overassessing the *Daybooks*. We must consider them the place where students are free to think things through, change their minds, even start over. But you can be alert to what the student is doing well, what is frustrating, what needs more time. To that end, we have provided a chart which may be useful in getting a sense of how students are progressing in using angles of literacy. By duplicating the chart for each student, you can track progress through the lessons. We would like to encourage the idea of jotting down notations as you work with students during the class period or look over the *Daybooks* after class. In this way, you can amass a sizable amount of information over a grading period. Coupled with a student self-assessment such as the one included here, you will have tangible evidence of achievement in the *Daybooks*.

STUDENT SELF-ASSESSMENT

A student self-assessment chart is a useful adjunct to the teacher chart. This particular format works well, as it asks students to consider interest, value, and participation as well as quality.

Followed by the self-assessment essay, it provides valuable insight into the student's sense of accomplishment.

INDIVIDUAL STUDENT EIGHT-WEEK ASSESSMENT CHART

The columns for each week's lessons can be used in different ways. We suggest the number system: a 5 for insightful, imaginative thinking or responding, a 1 for a minimal attempt. Some teachers prefer the check, check-plus, check-minus system. There is even room, if you turn the chart sideways, to make some notations.

Angles of Literacy

INTERACTING WITH A TEXT	I	II	III	IV	V	VI	VII	VIII
The student demonstrates understanding by using interactive strategies such as:								
underlining key phrases								
writing questions or comments in the margin								
noting word patterns and repetitions								
circling unknown words								
keeping track of ideas as they unfold								

MAKING CONNECTIONS	I	II	III	IV	V	VI	VII	VIII
The student makes connections to the stories with a text by:								
paying attention to the stories in the text								
connecting ideas and themes in the text to personal ideas, experience, feelings, and knowledge								
making connections to other texts, movies, television shows, or other media								

SHIFTING PERSPECTIVES	I	II	III	IV	V	VI	VII	VIII
The student is able to shift perspectives to examine a text from many points of view. When prompted, the student will engage in such strategies as:								
examining the point of view								
changing the point of view								
exploring various versions of an event, forming interpretations								
comparing texts and responding to "what if" questions to deepen understanding								

STUDYING THE LANGUAGE AND CRAFT OF A TEXT	I	II	III	IV	V	VI	VII	VIII
The student demonstrates an understanding of the way language and craft operate in a text. Specifically, the student will:								
show how imagery, metaphor, and figurative language are central to literature								
demonstrate an understanding of how an author's vocabulary and use of language are integral to the overall work								
use modeling to demonstrate an understanding of style and form								
demonstrate understanding of various genres and forms of literature								

FOCUSING ON THE WRITER	I	II	III	IV	V	VI	VII	VIII
The student demonstrates a rich understanding of a single writer's work, including:								
interpreting short texts by the author								
making inferences about the connections between an author's life and work								
analyzing the writer's style								
drawing conclusions about repeated themes and topics in an author's work								
evaluating a text or comparing works by the same author								

END OF TERM STUDENT SELF-ASSESSMENT CHART

Fill out the chart by naming or describing the work you have completed in the *Daybooks*. Since the *Daybooks* are focused on the reading of and writing about literature, it might be useful to list the actual texts you have read. To measure your achievement, think about the work you did as you explored the angles of vision for each text.

For each item, use the numbers 1 (low) to 5 (high) to indicate the four aspects of your involvement. Following completion of the chart, write the Self-Assessment Essay.

WORKS OF LITERATURE READ	LEVEL OF INTEREST	LEVEL OF VALUE	DEGREE OF PARTICIPATION	QUALITY OF PARTICIPATION

STUDENT SELF-ASSESSMENT ESSAY

After you have filled out this chart, write a self-evaluation essay, reflecting on your work in the *Daybooks* for the past term and articulating ideas about what you hope to achieve in the next. Refer specifically to the texts listed in the chart, elaborating on your assessment of a text's interest or value, commenting on reasons for the degree of your involvement, or explaining why you have assessed the quality of your work as you have.

Modeling: An Overview

by Fran Claggett

The overriding goal in modeling is to help students become discerning readers and inventive, perceptive writers. Modeling works well with students of all ability levels, whether homogeneously or heterogeneously grouped. It is especially effective in working with second-language students. My own classroom experience, as well as testimony from writers and researchers, indicates that modeling closely resembles the natural stages we go through in the acquisition of language. Many writers have talked about how, during their formative years, they either consciously or unconsciously imitated the styles of other writers whom they admired. Here, I will focus on the metacognitive aspects of modeling, making the processes of thinking and learning explicit for students, urging them to explore their own ways of making sense not only of what they read but what they write.

USING MODELING IN THE CLASSROOM

Through various modeling experiences, students learn the relationships among form, structure, and style. They learn to slow down their reading in order to appreciate the ways authors create specific effects. A critical aspect of using modeling with all students is the selection of the work to be modeled. The teacher must be clear on the focus of the assignment, allow for the margin of success by selecting works for modeling that are within the students' grasp, and make certain that students enter into the metacognitive aspect of the exercise.

Some of the ways that modeling can be integrated into classroom assignments:

1. As a catalyst for writing, particularly for reluctant writers. It immediately provides a structure and takes away much of the threat of the blank page.

2. As an introduction to poetry. Again, much of the onus is gone when students first model a poem, then discover the form by analyzing their own work as well as the original.

3. To encourage close reading of a text. As part of the study of a novel—particularly a difficult one stylistically—have students choose a representative passage (they decide what is representative), model it, then do a structural analysis of it. This exercise enhances both their understanding of the content of the original (it slows down their reading) and their grasp of the author's style. Students often work together in pairs or groups on this activity.

4. To teach awareness of diction. Choose a passage and, as a class, analyze its tone by exploring the use of diction, detail, and syntax. They might even write an analysis of the passage. Either after or before the analysis, students choose a different subject from that of the original and emulate the passage, working consciously to create a particular tone or effect. Students can also write emulations of each other's work, accompanied by an analysis and critique.

5. As a way of teaching English language sentence patterns to second-language learners. By modeling, students are able to internalize the natural flow of English sentences.

6. As part of an intensive author study. Students read a variety of works (short stories, essays, poems, novels, plays) by a single author. They select sections they believe to be representative of the author's style and analyze them from the standpoint of diction, tone, and main idea. They should model a short section. Their final piece in this assignment, which also involves secondary source biographical research, is to write a full imitation of the style of this author, showing through their choice of subject matter, genre, syntax, voice, and tone that they have developed and internalized a familiarity with the author's style.

KINDS OF MODELING TAUGHT IN THE DAYBOOKS

Emulation	replace word-for-word by function
Spinoff Modeling	respond to original content; retain tone, perhaps first line
Fixed Form Modeling	follow the pattern or form of the original (e.g., a sonnet)
Structural Modeling	model the thought progressions of the original
The Paralog	create a parallel dialogue with the author
Style Modeling	write a substantial piece in the style of an author

U n i t　　O v e r v i e w

In this unit, students will develop their abilities to annotate a text, make personal connections to what they read, examine perspectives, analyze an author's language, and reflect on knowledge of an author's life and works. As they read and respond to the poetry and nonfiction of Philip Larkin, students will improve their critical reading skills.

L i t e r a t u r e　　F o c u s

	Lesson	Literature
1.	Interacting With a Text	**Philip Larkin,** "Mother, Summer, I" (Poetry)
		Philip Larkin, "Far Out" (Poetry)
2.	Story Connections	**Philip Larkin,** "Ambulances" (Poetry)
3.	Shifting Perspectives	
4.	Language and Craft	**Philip Larkin,** "Street Lamps" (Poetry)
5.	Focus on the Writer	**Philip Larkin,** from "Notebooks" (Nonfiction)

R e a d i n g　　F o c u s

1. Active readers annotate the text, recording their reactions, questions, and other comments in the margins.
2. Readers can connect all the stories in a work of literature to their own life experiences.
3. Examine a piece of literature from several perspectives. Changes in point of view or "what if" speculations can change the interpretation of what you are reading.
4. Examining the use of language gives you clues about what the writer has chosen to emphasize and helps you see how craft supports meaning.
5. Examining a writer in depth—the author's life and work and what the author or others say about the work—is one way to extend your understanding of a literary selection.

W r i t i n g　　F o c u s

1. Write a paragraph describing your interpretation of a poem.
2. Describe a personal experience.
3. Examine a poem from different perspectives.
4. Explain how imagery contributes to the overall meaning of a poem.
5. Design a book cover, including a sketch and selected lines.

29

One Interacting With a Text

C r i t i c a l   R e a d i n g

FOCUS

Often in Philip Larkin's poetry, the speaker finds himself in a quandary, caught between alternative choices neither one of which is fully attractive to him.

BACKGROUND

Philip Larkin (1922–1985) came from a working-class background in the industrial north of England. He went to Oxford University. Many of his poems reflect the physical and human landscape of his past. In the first stanza of "Mother, Summer, I," Larkin compares a summer's day to a blanket that his mother shakes out suspiciously, always expecting to find trouble hidden within. In the second stanza, he reflects upon his own attitude toward sunny days and perfect happiness and admits that he, too, is more comfortable in "A time less bold, less rich, less clear: / An autumn more appropriate." In "Far Out," Larkin looks out into space beyond the familiar, comforting constellations and concludes that "Much less is known than not, / More far than near." There is much more of this universe that we don't know than there is of what we do.

FOR DISCUSSION AND REFLECTION

➤ Why do you think Larkin's mother loses her "worried summer look" when rains begin and the weather turns? (Answers should include discussion of how his mother is uncomfortable with the simple happiness of a summer's day and how she finds a rainy day a better match for her own inner climate.)

➤ What is Larkin saying in the second stanza about his own temperament? How is he like his mother and how is he different from her? (Although "summer-born / And summer-loving," Larkin admits that, like his mother, he feels unease in the "perfect happiness" of summer. He is more comfortable in the cold and dark of autumn.)

➤ Given what you have deduced regarding Larkin's temperament, how would you interpret his attitude in "Far Out"? (Many answers are possible but will likely focus on how the speaker is not satisfied with the simple "guidance or delight" that common star-gazing provides for most people and instead looks beyond the constellations to "darker spaces where / Small cloudy nests of stars / Seem to float on the air.")

W r i t i n g

QUICK ASSESS

Do students' paragraphs:

✓ offer an interpretation of "Far Out"?

✓ reflect a thoughtful reading of the poem?

Students are asked to write a paragraph describing their interpretations of "Far Out." Before they begin to write, make a cluster on the board of everything they know about star-gazing, constellations, and theories of the universe. Tapping their own prior knowledge about Larkin's subject may help them interpret the poem.

READING AND WRITING EXTENSIONS

➤ Have students write about a time when they looked up into the night sky for comfort, inspiration, or scientific exploration.

➤ Ask students to research theories and discoveries about what scientists have found exists "Far Out."

Two Story Connections

Critical Reading

FOCUS

Philip Larkin said, "Deprivation is for me what daffodils were for Wordsworth."

BACKGROUND

With the publication of his collection *The Less Deceived* in 1955, Philip Larkin established himself as the leader of the English anti-romantic movement, handling the old themes of childhood, love, and death with a searing wit and a sophisticated roughness of style and feeling. In "Ambulances," Larkin describes the passage of an ambulance through city streets: "Light glossy grey, arms on a plaque, / They come to rest at any kerb . . . ." Children and women stop to watch and as they do, "for a second get it whole, / So permanent and blank and true." They realize that an ambulance will one day come for them and those they love. The traffic stops to let the ambulance carrying its load pass by and in so doing "Brings closer what is left to come, / And dulls to distance all we are."

FOR DISCUSSION AND REFLECTION

➤ Why do you think ambulances give back "None of the glances they absorb"? (Many responses are possible. When people see an ambulance they wonder who is ill, who has had an accident, what tragedy has hit. The ambulance speeds by, answering no one.)

➤ What do the observers in the poem think about as they see the ambulance pass by? (The first thought is of sympathy for the person inside, but this soon shifts to a contemplation of their own mortality and the fragility of the lives of those they love.)

➤ How do you interpret Larkin's line "All streets in time are visited"? (The ambulance, a symbol of sickness and death, comes to every house and family eventually.)

Writing

QUICK ASSESS
Do students' descriptions:

✓ focus on a personal experience?

✓ identify a connection to "Ambulances"?

Students are asked to write about a time when an "ambulance" rode into the story of their own lives. It may help students to tell this story to a partner before they begin to write. Answering questions about what happened will help them to recall important details.

READING AND WRITING EXTENSIONS

➤ Read to students Emily Dickinson's poem "There's been a death in the opposite house" and ask them to compare this speaker's response to a neighbor's tragedy with the responses Larkin describes in "Ambulances."

➤ Have students write a narrative poem that uses as its title another kind of vehicle: police car, tanker truck, motorcycle, Volvo, horse trailer, fire engine, school bus, bulldozer.

Three Shifting Perspectives

Critical Reading

FOCUS
Point of view is the perspective from which a story is told.

BACKGROUND
A writer has a number of options to consider when deciding how to present events. The final effect is achieved through manipulation of character and plot. For this reason, the writer's most important technical decision may be which point of view to use. Point of view is determined by who is telling the story and the degree of knowledge possessed by the teller. "Mother, Summer, I" is told in the first person— the "I," the son, describing his mother's temperament and then his own. "Ambulances" is told from a third-person point of view. A detached narrator describes events and characters as an ambulance stops for an emergency and then speeds away. This lesson invites students to speculate about how shifting the perspective from which these stories are told would change their message and its effect on readers.

FOR DISCUSSION AND REFLECTION
➤ How do you think the mother in "Mother, Summer, I" might explain her own attitude toward fine weather? (Answers are likely to include speculation about what has happened in her life that has caused her to be pessimistic and to expect bad things lurking around the corner even when all the signs around her are sunny and bright.)

➤ How do you think the ambulance driver would describe the events in "Ambulances"? (For him, what happened would be all in a day's work, something he experienced all the time. It would not likely trigger reflection about his own mortality or the vulnerability of his loved ones.)

➤ What additional information would need to be provided in order to tell this story from the point of view of the sick or injured person? (Students are likely to suggest the nature of the injury or illness as well as the state of mind of the person on the stretcher. It would also be important to establish the person's age, sex, and feelings regarding the accident or disease.)

Writing

QUICK ASSESS
Do students' responses:

✓ discuss the effect of the title?

✓ explain how shifting the perspective in "Ambulances" would change the poem?

Students are asked to describe how they think they would react to "Ambulances" if it were told from the point of view of the ambulance driver and from the point of view of the person being driven to the hospital. It may help students to brainstorm together what they imagine would be going through the minds of these two characters during the course of the poem.

READING AND WRITING EXTENSIONS
➤ Have students write an interior monologue for one of the "children strewn on steps or road" watching the ambulance pass.

➤ Ask students to find other poems dealing with illness, accidents, or death. Have them compare the reflections of different narrators as they observe these difficult situations.

Four Language and Craft

Critical Reading

FOCUS

In his poem "Aubade," Larkin wrote, "I work all day, and get half drunk at night. / Waking at four to soundless dark. I stare."

BACKGROUND

Imagery in poetry may appeal to any of the senses. Visual images are the most common, but poets also look for ways to evoke sound, touch, and even smell and taste. Poets trust in the power of the depicted images to stand for or suggest moods and inner states. Ezra Pound founded a movement called Imagism, which championed short poems that were structured by a single image or metaphor and presented the reader an object or scene from the external world.

➤ In the first line of "Street Lamps," Philip Larkin uses a simile to compare the way the night changes with the movement of a puma, a large and predatory cat. Into this night emerge the street lamps. Larkin personifies the lamps. They "lean at corners," and one even leers "with a senile grin." In the final lines, Larkin suggests that this one defiant street lamp has the audacity to try to "cast shadows contrary to the sun."

FOR DISCUSSION AND REFLECTION

➤ What does the image of a puma suggest to you about Larkin's description of the night? (Responses are likely to include the fear often associated with the dark and the fear of a huge, predatory cat.)

➤ Given this portrayal of night, what purpose do the street lamps serve? (They provide the only light and "burn on, impersonal, through the night." They cast their own black shadows, "oblique and intense," through the long hours of the night.)

➤ What do you make of the one sole street lamp that burned on into the morning? (Students will probably identify this street lamp as a kind of rogue who dares to challenge the sun and just for fun tries to cast shadows toward the daylight.)

Writing

QUICK ASSESS

Do students' responses:

✓ draw on their charts and sketches?

✓ explain how the imagery contributes to the poem's meaning?

Students are asked to write about how the imagery in "Street Lamps" contributes to the overall meaning of the poem.

READING AND WRITING EXTENSIONS

➤ Have students read Larkin's poem "Aubade" and compare the imagery in it with that in "Street Lamps." Ask them to identify images that they find particularly effective.

➤ Invite students to take a man-made feature of the landscape—a stop sign, a billboard, a fire hydrant, a mailbox, a telephone pole—and write a prose description of it that uses different kinds of images to bring this object to life. Suggest that students use similes and metaphors.

Five Focus on the Writer

Critical Reading

FOCUS

From an early age, Philip Larkin knew that "What I was going to be praised and rewarded for—if anything—was writing."

BACKGROUND

Philip Larkin worked most of his life as a librarian. Appointed Librarian to the University of Hull in 1955, he presided over its transformation during the next two decades. Larkin received the Order of the Companion of Honour in 1985, though he was unable to accept it personally owing to the onset of a terminal illness. He died of cancer on December 1, 1985, at age 63. Larkin's *Collected Poems* was published in October 1988. The publication of his *Selected Letters* in 1992 and Andrew Motion's *Philip Larkin, A Writer's Life* in 1993 caused a furor in literary circles because they revealed many of the author's privately expressed animosities and prejudices. Larkin's poetry, however stern and even bleak its viewpoint often is, demonstrates a unique combination of colloquial ease and metrical finesse, humor, and candor.

FOR DISCUSSION AND REFLECTION

➤ Based upon this excerpt, how would you explain Philip Larkin's home life? (Encourage students to speculate on how the daily behaviors Larkin describes would be likely to affect relationships between the mother, father, sister, and Philip.)

➤ What generalization can you draw from Larkin's statement that "I don't think my father liked working or gardening, I don't think my mother liked keeping house, I don't think my sister liked living at home"? (Answers are likely to include the speculation that Larkin sees so much personal unhappiness around him that he is determined that his own life should not be so circumscribed by unhappiness.)

➤ How did Philip Larkin know that what he "was going to be praised and rewarded for—if anything—was writing"? (He had begun to realize that he would never excel in sports or languages or science, but teachers used his writing as a model for other students. This gave him the inkling that writing was his "element.")

Writing

QUICK ASSESS

Do students' book covers:

✓ include a title and cover design on the front?

✓ include creative copy and sample lines on the back?

Students are asked to design a book cover for one of Larkin's works. Have them look at a selection of other books of poetry or autobiography to see what publishers typically include on covers. Invite students to write creative copy for the back that would induce readers to buy this volume.

READING AND WRITING EXTENSIONS

➤ Read students Larkin's poem "Home Is So Sad" and discuss how its theme compares with the excerpt from "Notebooks."

➤ Have students describe what they think they will be "praised and rewarded for" in their lives.

BUILDING AN INTERPRETATION

Unit Overview

In "Building an Interpretation," students are invited to explore the various levels of meaning in the texts they read. By focusing on how writers develop their subject through using conflicts, creating tone, and selecting imagery, students develop their abilities to build interpretations of their own.

Literature Focus

	Lesson	Literature
1.	Subject and Story Meaning	**Roddy Doyle,** from *Paddy Clarke Ha Ha Ha* (Novel)
2.	Conflict and Story Meaning	**William Trevor,** from "The Piano Tuner's Wives" (Short Story)
3.	Conveying Meaning Through Tone	
4.	Imagery and Meaning	**David Malouf,** from *The Conversations at Curlow Creek* (Novel)
5.	Interpreting Meaning	

Reading Focus

1. Readers need to compare the story subject to their own lives, examine how the writer develops the subject, and generalize from the story events in order to build an interpretation.

2. The conflicts presented in a story dramatize key themes that can be interpreted for what they contribute to the overall meaning of a story.

3. Understanding the tone used to describe the subject and characters in a story is one way of developing an interpretation about the story's meaning.

4. In developing an interpretation, it is important to monitor your responses to the imagery and to examine how particular images emphasize the story's meaning.

5. Interpreting involves looking closely at a combination of characteristics and impressions from a story and then piecing together their meaning.

Writing Focus

1. Answer questions about an excerpt from a novel.
2. Complete a chart about a story's conflicts.
3. Vary the tone of a story.
4. Describe how particular images contribute to a work's overall meaning.
5. Write a short interpretive essay.

One Subject and Story Meaning

Critical Reading

FOCUS

Paddy Clarke Ha Ha Ha charts the triumphs, indignities, and bewilderment of a ten-year-old boy growing up in Ireland.

BACKGROUND

Roddy Doyle was born in Dublin in 1958 and taught school there for fourteen years. His first three novels—*The Commitments, The Snapper,* and *The Van*—offer the continuing story of the cheerfully irreverent Rabbitte family. Though similar in setting and style, *Paddy Clarke Ha Ha Ha* is a much darker tale. In this excerpt from the novel, Paddy Clarke's teacher, Miss Watkins, brings to class a commemorative dishtowel celebrating the fiftieth anniversary of Irish Independence. The proclamation read, "We declare the right of the people of Ireland to the ownership of Ireland and to the unfettered control of Irish destinies, to be sovereign and indefeasible." The signers of this document had decided that British involvement in World War I was sufficient distraction to provide the Irish a chance to gain their full independence. This led to the failed Easter Rebellion in 1916. The British imprisoned hundreds of rebels and executed the leaders.

FOR DISCUSSION AND REFLECTION

➤ Why do you think Miss Watkins chose to bring in the tea towel to show to her students? (Discussion is likely to focus on how she wants to teach the boys about Irish history as well as her own passion for the cause.)

➤ How do you interpret Paddy's response to the lesson? (Paddy is distracted from the history lesson by the sight of his own name "Clarke" on the towel. This causes him to think of his own grandfather. Because he doesn't quite know what to do with these memories—and because he is a typical ten-year-old boy—he chooses to disrupt the class by pretending that the signer of the declaration was his "Granda Clarke.")

➤ What does Miss Watkins's response to the disruption tell you about her? (Many responses are possible but should include her determination that the boys should know Irish history and respect the memory of those who have died in pursuit of independence.)

Writing

QUICK ASSESS

Do students' answers:

✓ compare the incidents and characters with their own experiences?

✓ comment on various techniques that Doyle uses to influence readers?

✓ explain which ideas seem significant?

Students are asked to write about the ideas that seem significant in this story. Begin by identifying what students feel are key moments in the scene and then have them discuss with a partner why they feel the line or incident is important to the story's meaning.

READING AND WRITING EXTENSIONS

➤ Have students write about a time when they got in trouble in elementary school. Suggest that they not interpret the story they tell, just describe the incident in detail.

➤ Ask students to read the novel *Paddy Clarke Ha Ha Ha* and then discuss why students think Roddy Doyle chose to tell this story from the point of view of a young boy rather than from the perspective of an adult or an omniscient narrator.

Two Conflict and Story Meaning

Critical Reading

FOCUS

William Trevor introduces conflict in his third sentence when his narrator explains that "in choosing Violet to be his wife the piano tuner had rejected Belle, which was something everyone remembered . . . ."

BACKGROUND

William Trevor was born in Mitchelstown, County Cork, in 1928, and spent his childhood in provincial Ireland. He attended a number of Irish schools and later Trinity College, Dublin. Many of his stories have appeared in *The New Yorker* and other magazines. In 1977, Trevor was made an honorary Commander of the British Empire in recognition of his services to literature. In this excerpt from "The Piano Tuner's Wives," William Trevor introduces his main characters and the source of conflict in the story. Conflict creates tension and suspense and is the heart of a story. External conflict occurs when a central character is at odds with another person, with a system of beliefs, with the gods, or with natural forces. Internal conflict occurs when a character is at war with himself or herself.

FOR DISCUSSION AND REFLECTION

➤ How might a blind man's choice of a wife be different from the choice he would make if he could see? (Answers will vary but are likely to include discussion of the dependence that he will always have upon his mate. Point students to the line where the piano tuner is shaking hands after the ceremony, "seeing in his mental eye faces that his first wife had described for him.")

➤ How does Belle explain to herself the piano tuner's choice of an older, less attractive wife over herself? (She decides that he chose on the basis of convenience and material gain: "he had preferred Violet—or the prospect of the house that would one day become hers . . . and the little bit of money there was, an easement in a blind man's existence.")

➤ Why do you think it irritated Belle when people called the piano tuner Violet's child? (Many responses are possible, but they should include speculation that Belle believes Violet contributed to this perception of the man by encouraging his dependence.)

Writing

QUICK ASSESS

Do students' responses:

✓ identify a variety of conflicts in the story?

✓ discriminate between external and internal conflict?

✓ include specific reasons for their thinking?

Students are asked to chart the conflicts in the story and determine whether they are internal or external.

READING AND WRITING EXTENSIONS

➤ Have students finish reading "The Piano Tuner's Wives" and then discuss how the hints of conflict were developed in the story.

➤ Ask students to imagine they are Belle. Have them write a diary entry from the night before the wedding in which she expresses her hopes and concerns for the future.

Three Conveying Meaning Through Tone

Critical Reading

FOCUS

Tone is the emotional coloring that reveals a writer's attitude toward the subject and toward the reader. It ranges from light or frivolous to bitter or gloomy.

BACKGROUND

Tone is directly related to point of view. How the story is told depends on who is telling it and has everything to do with the narrator's relation to the events. Remind students that third-person narration automatically presumes a certain degree of objectivity. In "The Piano Tuner's Wives," William Trevor has chosen to employ a third-person narrator who, though calm and detached, seems to have an interest in Belle's welfare.

FOR DISCUSSION AND REFLECTION

➤ Is "The Piano Tuner's Wives" told in a neutral, straightforward voice, or does the narrator's tone convey a particular attitude toward the characters and events? (The tone of this story suggests that things will not go well for Belle in her new marriage. Have students find places in the story where this is suggested.)

➤ What does the narrator's use of direct quotations from townspeople suggest to readers? (Answers should include mention that the narrator seems to be an insider who has known the piano tuner, Violet, and Belle for a long time. There is a familiarity to the tone.)

➤ With what overall feeling does reading this opening to "The Piano Tuner's Wives" leave you? (Many responses are possible, but they are likely to include a sense of foreboding for what will happen in this marriage.)

Writing

QUICK ASSESS

Do students' descriptions:

✓ reflect understanding of the narrator's tone?

✓ recast Trevor's descriptions using a different tone?

Students are asked to choose one subject from "The Piano Tuner's Wives" and explain the tone Trevor uses to describe it. They are then asked to rewrite this description using a different tone. Have students consider the features of the new tone that they are trying to achieve before they begin to write.

READING AND WRITING EXTENSIONS

➤ Read to students from the opening of William Trevor's novel *Felicia's Journey* and discuss together how tone contributes to their initial impression of this fictional world: "She keeps being sick. A woman in the washroom says: 'You'd be better off in the fresh air. Wouldn't you go up on the deck?' It's cold on the deck and the wind hurts her ears. When she has been sick over the rail she feels better and goes downstairs again, to where she was sitting before she went to the washroom. The clothes she picked out for her journey are in two green carrier bags; the money is in her handbag."

➤ Have students write two congratulatory notes to Belle on the occasion of her wedding: one using a tone that conveys genuine happiness for the newlyweds, another using a tone that conveys reservations on the part of the writer regarding the future.

Four Imagery and Meaning

Critical Reading

FOCUS

David Malouf uses imagery to recreate the world that his characters carry in their heads "which was infinitely expandable and had nothing to do with the movements of either the earth or the sun."

BACKGROUND

Imagery consists of words and phrases that recreate sensory experiences for a reader. Though images are often visual, some appeal to the reader's sense of smell, hearing, taste, or touch. Australian poet and novelist David Malouf is a master of imagery. Malouf began his career as a poet, publishing several respected volumes, but he is best known for his fiction, which incorporates his poetic gift for observation and description. The novel from which this excerpt was taken, *The Conversations at Curlow Creek,* was nominated for the 1997 Miles Franklin Award.

FOR DISCUSSION AND REFLECTION

➤ Draw symbols for the five senses on the board and ask students to find images from the excerpt that appeal to each of them. Help students to notice how some images appeal to more than one sense—for example, "Its surface rippled like silk, and the whole weight and light of it was sucked upwards in a single movement that took his breath away . . . ."

➤ Have you ever had dreams like this that seemed to be long and involved yet in fact involved only moments of sleep? (Many responses are possible. Draw students' attention to the lines in the excerpt where Malouf talks about this relativity of dreamtime.)

➤ Based upon his dream and his exchange with his companion, what kind of a man do you think Adair is? (Answers are likely to include discussion of his powerful imagination, his wariness, his philosophical bent, his interest in the natural world as a source of meaning.)

Writing

QUICK ASSESS

Do students' responses:

✓ offer an assertion about the imagery in Adair's dream?

✓ list specific imagery as support?

✓ explain why the imagery is important?

Students are asked to determine what they believe the imagery in Adair's dream suggests and then to list imagery from the text that supports their interpretation. There are many possible interpretations of this imagery, and it may help to put several of these on the board so that students are not working from the mistaken assumption that there is one correct interpretation.

READING AND WRITING EXTENSIONS

➤ Have students read William Wordsworth's "Lines Composed a Few Miles Above Tintern Abbey" and compare his use of imagery with that of David Malouf. Explain, for example, that the lines "These waters, rolling from their mountain-springs / With a soft inland murmur" appeal to two senses—sight and hearing.

➤ Ask students to describe a dream of their own—real or imagined—that was full of sensory images.

Five Interpreting Meaning

Critical Reading

FOCUS

Poetic and powerful, *The Conversations at Curlow Creek* takes place over just one night.

BACKGROUND

The Conversations at Curlow Creek take place in 1827. In a remote hut on the high plains of New South Wales, two strangers spend the night in talk. One, Carney—an illiterate Irishman, ex-convict and bushranger—is to be hanged at dawn. The other, Adair, is the soldier who has been sent out to supervise the hanging. As the night wears on, the two men share memories and uncover unlikely connections in their lives.

FOR DISCUSSION AND REFLECTION

➤ What do you think the images in Adair's dream tell you about his mental state? (Students are likely to see the birds as symbolizing flight and escape.)

➤ What does the line "He knew this country well enough by now to be skeptical of his senses" suggest to you about Adair? (Answers will likely include mention that Adair is currently far from his native land and has adopted a wary stance toward his surroundings. A later line, "It is a door in the darkness, a way out," suggests that he feels trapped here.)

➤ How do you interpret Adair's perception of Carney's gaze upon him as "intense, almost predatory"? (Adair seems both to fear Carney and to see him as someone who can explain his dream, "as if he might have news to bring him out of what he had dreamed.")

Writing

QUICK ASSESS

Do students' essays:

✔ explain the meaning of the story?

✔ offer text specifics as support?

Students are asked to write an interpretive essay about this episode from *The Conversations at Curlow Creek*. In order to help them focus their essays, have students generate a thesis statement that clearly demonstrates what they think about the piece. Then they should collect evidence that supports this interpretation from the text.

READING AND WRITING EXTENSIONS

➤ Read students Annie Dillard's essay "Mirages" from her book *Teaching a Stone to Talk* and have them compare her use of imagery with that of Malouf: "All summer long mirages appear and vanish. While they last they mince and maul the island and waters, and put us in thrall to our senses. It is as though summer itself were a mirage, a passive dream of pleasure, itself untrue. For in winter the beaches lie empty . . . ."

➤ Have students choose words or phrases from *The Conversations at Curlow Creek* and assemble them into a found poem.

Unit Overview

In this unit, students will focus on how writers make their fictional worlds seem believable to readers. Students consider works by Penelope Trevor, Nadine Gordimer, and Salman Rushdie. They will understand the strategies writers use to make their characters and plots convincing.

Literature Focus

	Lesson	Literature
1.	How Readers Come to Believe	**Penelope Trevor,** from *Listening for Small Sounds* (Novel)
2.	Creating Believability	**Nadine Gordimer,** "Comrades" (Short Story)
3.	Writing Unwritten Scenes	
4.	Believing the Fantastic	**Salman Rushdie,** from "An Iff and a Butt" from *Haroun and the Sea of Stories* (Novel)
5.	Creating a Believable Fantasy	

Reading Focus

1. Believability in a story develops from concrete details that present events and characters.
2. Consider the believability of characters by examining their actions, their characteristics, and the ending of the story.
3. By writing unwritten scenes, readers fill in missing perspectives, provide background information, or create a version of events to better understand the situation.
4. A story with fantastic elements creates its own "facts" that push the reader to suspend disbelief and enter the world created by the writer.
5. Sometimes writers break readers' expectations of how a story gets told. Instead they create a different type of believability that will engage the readers' imaginations.

Writing Focus

1. Analyze the details that make a story believable.
2. Describe how believable you find a story's ending.
3. Write a scene, in the style of Gordimer, that could be added to her story.
4. Explain selected facts from a fantasy story.
5. Write a fantasy that blends two fairy tales.

One How Readers Come to Believe

Critical Reading

FOCUS

Sven Birkerts on fictional writing:

"Fiction is a weaving together of two very different strands—one pulling the reader away from the world of daily cares, the other pulling him toward that world."

BACKGROUND

In this excerpt from *Listening for Small Sounds,* Penelope Trevor describes an exchange between a mother cleaning the bathroom and her nine-year-old daughter. Students may at first be puzzled by the opening sentence about the coming of spring—"September winds blow away the grey and the sun rises, yellow, into a blue sky"—until you explain that below the equator, in Australia, the seasons are the opposite of ours. Joss brings her mother a bitter mandarin orange as an offering and then proceeds to talk to her in the self-obsessed way that precocious young children have. The mother is preoccupied. Both the scrubbing and the knitting seem to be ways of keeping her hands busy while her mind is on other things.

FOR DISCUSSION AND REFLECTION

➤ Why do you think the mother replies so sparingly to the girl's comments and questions? (Many responses are possible but will likely include discussion of Joss as a chatterbox who probably talks nonstop all the time. Students should speculate on the mother's preoccupation and lack of appetite.)

➤ What possible reason might the mother have for scrubbing the bath tiles that "don't look dirty to Joss"? (The mother seems to be creating work for herself in order to give her hands something to do. This may be a way to avoid thinking too much. The final paragraph describing the mother knitting also supports this suggestion.)

➤ Can you remember your mother or father ever behaving this way when you were a child? In retrospect, can you think of reasons why they may have seemed preoccupied? (Answers will vary.)

Writing

QUICK ASSESS

Do students' paragraphs:

✓ describe the part of the episode that they found most convincing?

✓ analyze concrete details as support for their judgment?

Students are asked to describe the part of the episode that they think is developed most convincingly. In order to help students visualize the events in this excerpt, it may be useful to turn the text into a reader's theater script and have students act out what is happening for the class.

READING AND WRITING EXTENSIONS

➤ Invite students to imagine what they think the mother in this episode is preoccupied with. Have them write her interior monologue as Joss tells her about creating a vaccine.

➤ Ask students to recall children's books and stories that have main characters like Joss, competent and confident young girls eager to take on life. Their responses might include *Harriet the Spy* by Louise Fitzhugh, *Matilda* by Roald Dahl, and *Little Women* by Louisa May Alcott.

Two Creating Believability

Critical Reading

FOCUS

Gordimer has said that "I live at 6,000 feet in a society whirling, stamping, swaying with the force of revolutionary change."

BACKGROUND

Nadine Gordimer is a South African writer whose work is largely concerned with the political situation in her native land. A consummate stylist, Gordimer writes with precision and integrity about a society divided by racist policies. Her firm opposition to the cruelty and injustice of apartheid is imparted not through polemic but through psychological insight and careful irony. In 1991, Nadine Gordimer was awarded the Nobel Prize in Literature. Before having students read "Comrades," you may want to tap students' prior knowledge about apartheid in South Africa. In this story, a well-intentioned white lady, Mrs. Hattie Telford, offers first a ride and then a meal to a group of young black men who had traveled a long way to attend a university conference on People's Education. Though she and they are "comrades" in the cause for justice, the enormous differences in their respective life experiences mean that all people will need education for a new South Africa to work.

FOR DISCUSSION AND REFLECTION

➤ Why do you think Hattie stops for Dumile? (There are many reasons for her behavior. Her presence at the conference suggests her support for people like these young men. Dumile has addressed her as "Comrade." She lives with a sense of guilt for all the advantages that she has that others go without.)

➤ What are the sources of discomfort between Hattie and the young men? (Answers are likely to include a distrust on both sides for someone of another race, Hattie's awareness of how her house and maid may appear to the young men, the young men's hunger and unfamiliarity with the kind of life Hattie's dining room represents.)

➤ As Hattie asks the young men about their education, what does she begin to realize about her questions? (She realizes how the revolution has consumed the years they should have been able to spend in school and how the time they have spent in prison and will continue to spend in the struggle for freedom will never allow them the luxury of education.)

Writing

QUICK ASSESS
Do students' descriptions:

✔ analyze the believability of the story's ending?

✔ include text specifics as support?

Students are asked to write about the believability of the ending. Before they begin to write, discuss the final paragraph of the story, making sure students understand the last line: "Only the food that fed their hunger was real."

READING AND WRITING EXTENSIONS

➤ Have students read "Safe Houses," from Nadine Gordimer's collection *Jump*. The story recounts a short-lived, intense affair between a revolutionary in hiding and a suburban socialite.

➤ Invite students to write about a time when they were in surroundings so unfamiliar to them that they could hardly speak or behave normally. This could be the first day at a new school, a trip to a foreign country, or a visit to a relative.

Three Writing Unwritten Scenes

Critical Reading

FOCUS

From Nadine Gordimer's novel *None to Accompany Me*:

"When every old distinction of privilege is defeated and abolished, there comes an aristocracy of those in danger. All feel diminished, outclassed in their company."

BACKGROUND

Nadine Gordimer was born in a small town near Johannesburg, South Africa. Uninspired by her education at a convent school, she turned to books at an early age. Gordimer was greatly influenced by the work of D. H. Lawrence, Henry James, and Ernest Hemingway. From their prose, as well as from her own highly developed skills as an observer, she honed a realistic style that has allowed her to fashion psychologically complex assessments of life in her native land. Gordimer explores not only the conflicts between black and white cultures but also the many strategies of compromise and coexistence.

FOR DISCUSSION AND REFLECTION

➤ Before students can begin to think about writing an unwritten scene for this story, they will need to analyze both its structure and Gordimer's style. What point of view has Gordimer chosen for her story? (The story is told in a limited third-person voice. The narrator has access to Hattie's thoughts and feelings but not to those of the young men.)

➤ How would you characterize Nadine Gordimer's sentences? (They are often exceedingly complex. Draw students' attention to such sentences as, "The spokesman, Dumile, tells her he wants to study by correspondence, 'get his matric' that he was preparing for two years ago; two years ago when he was still a child, when he didn't have the hair that is now appearing on his face, making him a man, taking away the childhood.")

➤ What effect do these long, generative sentences have upon the reader? (Answers should include discussion of how such sentences allow a writer to develop complex ideas. The sentence's meaning seems to build with each additional descriptive phrase or clause. Readers need to stay focused and pay attention in order not to get lost along the way.)

Writing

QUICK ASSESS

Do students' scenes:

✓ imitate Gordimer's style?

✓ reflect understanding of the story?

Students are asked to write an additional scene for "Comrades." Have students map the events in this story using a storyboard to help them decide where an additional scene could be added.

READING AND WRITING EXTENSIONS

➤ Have students read Nadine Gordimer's essay "Letter from Johannesburg" (1976), which describes in detail the Soweto riots. Encourage students to compare Gordimer's nonfiction style with her fictional style.

➤ Ask students to write Hattie's diary entry for the day she met Dumile and his comrades. What do students think Hattie may have learned from this experience?

Four Believing the Fantastic

Critical Reading

FOCUS

From *Haroun and the Sea of Stories*:

"Anybody can tell stories. Liars, and cheats, and crooks, for example. But for stories with that Extra Ingredient, ah, for those, even the best storytellers need the Story Waters. Storytelling needs fuel."

BACKGROUND

Salman Rushdie's novel *Haroun and the Sea of Stories* is a fantasy which, like many other magical realist stories, has a strong narrative drive. The recognizably realistic mingles with the unexpected and the inexplicable. Elements of dreams, fairy tales, and mythology combine with everyday objects and occurrences. In many ways, the book is an adventure novel about a son's attempt to rescue his father and return to him his Gift of Gab. Iff, a water genie, and Butt, a mad bus driver, assist Haroun in his quest.

FOR DISCUSSION AND REFLECTION

➤ Iff tells Haroun that the Ocean of the Streams of Story is like a library and unlike a library. What sense do you make of this? (The Ocean is like a library because it contains so many stories from all over the universe, but unlike a library of books, the stories in the Ocean are alive.)

➤ How does Iff persuade Haroun to take a swig from the Ocean of the Streams of Story? (Iff flatters the boy by telling him that "if you are very, very careful, or very, very highly skilled, you can dip a cup into the Ocean . . . ." He tells Haroun that it will cheer him up and make him feel "A-number-one.")

➤ Why do you think that Haroun was "beginning to wish he'd stayed in his peacock bed"? (Answers should include Haroun's reluctance to get involved in something that was becoming extremely complicated and full of unfamiliar things.)

Writing

QUICK ASSESS

Do students' responses:

✓ identify facts that readers are asked to believe?

✓ explain the importance of the passages they select?

Students are asked to identify facts that they must believe to accept the story and then to explain why these passages are important. Discuss how the tone helps the reader suspend his or her disbelief.

READING AND WRITING EXTENSIONS

➤ Have students read more of *Haroun and the Sea of Stories* by Salman Rushdie and discuss why they believe stories are so important to us.

➤ Tell students the ancient Chinese folktale of Mulan, read them Maxine Hong Kingston's version of this story in *The Woman Warrior*, and invite them to view the Disney movie *Mulan*. Have students write about the transformation of this folktale in the light of Iff's statement that "because the stories were held here in fluid form, they retained the ability to change, to become new versions of themselves."

Five Creating a Believable Fantasy

Critical Reading

FOCUS

From Alison Lurie's review of *Haroun and the Sea of Stories*:

"Mr. Rushdie's puns and anagrams, and his exuberant wordplay suggest *Alice in Wonderland* and Norton Juster's *Phantom Tollbooth*."

BACKGROUND

Salman Rushdie wrote *Haroun and the Sea of Stories* while himself in captivity. In February 1989, Ayatollah Ruhollah Khomeini of Iran announced that for writing *The Satanic Verses*, Salman Rushdie and "all involved in its publication who were aware of its content" were sentenced to death. From that moment to this, Rushdie has lived in hiding. *Haroun and the Sea of Stories* was dedicated to his son, Zafar: "Zembla, Zenda, Xanadu: / All our dream-worlds may come true. / Fairy lands are fearsome too. / As I wander far from view / Read and bring me home to you." Rushdie has written of his exile that he feels he has been plunged, like Alice, into the world beyond the looking-glass where nonsense is the only available sense.

FOR DISCUSSION AND REFLECTION

➤ Why do you imagine Rushdie named Haroun's guide and mentor "Iff"? (The name is a play on *if* and suggests the "what if" nature of fantasy stories. Iff educates Haroun about the Ocean of the Streams of Story.)

➤ What do you think is the significance of having Haroun turn from hero to monster in the water-induced story? (Iff wanted Haroun to experience the pleasure of playing the hero, but with the Ocean of the Streams of Story polluted, it turns into a nightmare.)

➤ Based upon what you know about stories, what do you think will happen next in this one? (In hero stories, it is very common for a formidable enemy to be identified; here it is Khattam-Shud: "Far away on the horizon, forked lightning glittered, once. Haroun felt his blood run cold." Haroun senses that this is the beginning of a problem he will play a part in solving, a monster he must vanquish.)

Writing

QUICK ASSESS

Do students' stories:

✓ choose two fairy tales to combine?

✓ reflect Rushdie's ideas of a "polluted story"?

Students are asked to take two familiar fairy tales and create a "polluted" version by combining them in unexpected ways. It will help students to brainstorm a long list of fairy tales on the board so that they have many stories to choose from.

READING AND WRITING EXTENSIONS

➤ Have students read Salman Rushdie's essay "In Good Faith," in which Rushdie offers an explanation for why he wrote *The Satanic Verses*.

➤ Ask students to imagine they are parents and then have them write a fantasy story that they would like to tell their children at bedtime.

Unit Overview

In this unit, as they read a variety of nonfiction, students will develop strategies to help them understand and appreciate writing about unfamiliar subjects. Among topics included are considering the author's attitude and inner conflicts, examining realistic and imaginary details, and establishing points of reference.

Literature Focus

	Lesson	Literature
1.	Considering Sources	**Paul Theroux,** from "Subterranean Gothic" (Nonfiction)
2.	Identifying Inner Conflict	**Jonathan Raban,** from "Sea-Room" (Nonfiction)
3.	Real and Imaginary Details	**Jonathan Raban,** from "Sea-Room" (Nonfiction)
4.	Point of View	**Evelyn Waugh,** "American Tourists in Egypt" from *Labels: A Mediterranean Journey* (Nonfiction)
5.	Establishing Points of Reference	**Isabel Fonseca,** from *Bury Me Standing* (Nonfiction)

Reading Focus

1. Consider the sources of information, including the author's attitude toward the subject, when reading descriptions of an unfamiliar subject.
2. Movement in an essay can come from the author's inner tensions and conflicts. Watch for descriptions of differences between the writer and his dreams.
3. Pay attention to both the realistic and imaginary details in a travel text. They will give you clues about how the writer sees himself and his journey.
4. Writers of satire reveal through their point of view the weaknesses or flaws in human beings. When reading satire, it is important to pay attention to the contrasting details the writer uses.
5. Establish your own points of reference when reading about unfamiliar subjects. Notice key details and make comparisons to what you do know.

Writing Focus

1. Analyze details that indicate the author's attitude toward his subjects.
2. Describe the inner conflicts in an author's life.
3. Complete a chart about realistic and imaginary details in an excerpt of nonfiction.
4. List words and phrases that indicate a satiric purpose.
5. Analyze an author's use of details.

One Considering Sources

Critical Reading

FOCUS

There are travel writers who make you wish you were "there," and there are travel writers so good at evoking a place that you almost are "there" without going.

BACKGROUND

As a travel writer, Paul Theroux has raised disenchantment with exotic places to an art form. He is a master of the drab and forlorn. He has explored the remote, rough corners of the complex, troubled nations of Africa, Asia, and Central and South America. His books include *The Great Railway Bazaar, The Old Patagonian Express,* and *The Pillars of Hercules.* In this excerpt from his essay "Subterranean Gothic," Theroux describes his experience of riding the New York City subway. His reference to "O dark dark dark. They all go into the dark" is from a hymn that is itself taken from Milton's *Samson Agonistes:* "On dark, dark, dark, amid the blaze of noon, / Irrecoverably dark, total eclipse / Without all hope of day!"

FOR DISCUSSION AND REFLECTION

➤ Why do you think Theroux titled his essay "Subterranean Gothic"? (*Subterranean* means under ground. *Gothic* refers literally to the style of architecture common in western Europe during medieval times. The word has many connotations, and students are most likely to recall Gothic novels, which are characterized by horror, violence, supernatural effects and dark, gloomy settings. Theroux is suggesting that the subway of New York City shares these features.)

➤ What do you think Theroux is suggesting when he says that "there is more Original Sin among subway passengers"? (Many responses are possible, but students may mention the guilt subway riders seem to be born with. The passengers look as though they are guilty of unmentionable crimes.)

➤ What does Theroux achieve by comparing the New York City subway with San Francisco's BART? (Answers should include reference to the way New Yorkers' lives are different from San Franciscans' lives.)

Writing

QUICK ASSESS

Do students' responses:

✓ describe Theroux's attitude toward Americans?

✓ draw on specifics from the text?

Students are asked to write about Theroux's attitude toward Americans. Make a list together on the board of all the places in "Subterranean Gothic" where Theroux drops hints concerning his attitude.

READING AND WRITING EXTENSIONS

➤ Have students read *The Pillars of Hercules*, Theroux's account of the most unpleasant hotels, ferries, cities, and people around the Mediterranean basin. Ask students to consider why this might be called an "anti-guidebook."

➤ Ask students to use Theroux's piece as a model for writing an "anti-guidebook" for a place they know well. Encourage them to include vivid details as Theroux has in "Subterranean Gothic."

Two Identifying Inner Conflict

Critical Reading

FOCUS

Jonathan Raban has sailed alone around Britain and spent a great deal of time on the coastal seas of Europe. He now lives in Seattle, where he sails a twenty-year-old Swedish ketch on the rim of the North Pacific.

BACKGROUND

In this excerpt from "Sea-Room," Jonathan Raban explores the theme of running away to sea as a way to explain both to himself and to his readers his own need to leave home. He begins by comparing this longing with "a nervous itch" that would not go away. He then describes the imaginary sailor who haunts him: "Lucky man. He'd slung his hook, and upped and gone." Raban then recalls heroes from literature who are "always running away to sea" because the voyage is "more than an adventure; it is a rite of passage . . . ." What Raban envied most from these heroes' stories was the farewell letters. He wishes he could borrow their language to write one of his own.

FOR DISCUSSION AND REFLECTION

➤ Why do you think Jonathan Raban chose to open his essay with a quote from *Moby Dick?* (Students may respond that Melville's novel is the classic American sea story and that Melville's narrator, Ishmael, explains why he feels "it high time to get to sea.")

➤ What do Raban's references to heroes in literature suggest to you about his character? (Many responses are possible, but students are likely to infer that Raban has read a great deal and identifies with these fictional young men who can wake up one morning and say, "Goodbye, family! Goodbye, friends! Goodbye, England!")

➤ How might a sea voyage be a "rite of passage, as decisive as a wedding"? (Embarking on a sea voyage means that an individual has decided to break with the world of home and enter the world of adults. Childhood and dependency are left behind.)

Writing

QUICK ASSESS

Do students' responses:

✓ describe the tensions and conflict in Raban's life?

✓ identify appropriate passages in the text?

Before students write about the tensions and conflict in Raban's life, suggest that they list words and images that describe the kind of person they imagine Jonathan Raban to be.

READING AND WRITING EXTENSIONS

➤ Have students write about a time when they dreamed of escaping the familiar world of their homes. Where did they imagine they would go?

➤ Read students Alfred Lord Tennyson's "Crossing the Bar" and ask them to compare this narrator's attitude toward setting out to sea with that of Raban. As Tennyson writes, "Sunset and evening star, / And one clear call for me! / And may there be no moaning of the bar, / When I put out to sea."

Three Real and Imaginary Details

Critical Reading

BACKGROUND

Successful travel literature depends largely upon the wit, powers of observation, and character of the traveler for its success. In past centuries, the traveler tended to be an adventurer or a connoisseur of art, landscapes, or strange customs who may also have been a writer. Contemporary travel literature is similarly as much about the author as it is about the territory described. In another excerpt from "Sea-Room," the reader can feel Jonathan Raban's desire to escape his current life in the way he constructs an imaginary boat from the details he learns about real boats: "As I came to put names to all its parts, the boat in my head grew more substantial and particular by the day."

FOR DISCUSSION AND REFLECTION

➤ What does Raban mean when he writes in the second paragraph that "running away is really a means of coming home"? (Answers are likely to include discussion of the fact that things had become intolerable for Raban at home. He "didn't much care for the appearance of this new day." By leaving a place that was stifling him, Raban was actually returning to a place where he could thrive and grow.)

➤ Why do you think Raban becomes obsessed with boats? (Boats may represent adventure, travel, and escape.)

➤ Why do you think Raban describes Ladbroke Grove and Notting Hill as "confused seas" in the final paragraph? (Many responses are possible, but students should see that Raban is speaking metaphorically here. Things are confused for him at home, and he imagines that his dream ship will be able to carry him safely away from these troubled waters.)

Writing

Students are asked to chart the features of real boats and the features of Raban's imaginary boat. Before they begin to write, ask two volunteers to take the parts of a boat salesman and Jonathan Raban. Have them ad lib a conversation that might occur on the dock.

READING AND WRITING EXTENSIONS

➤ Read to students from *The Yangtze Valley and Beyond*, Isabella Bird's journal of her travels in China in 1896 when she was sixty-four years old. Have students compare her Victorian style of travel writing with that of Paul Theroux and Jonathan Raban.

➤ Have students write a dialogue between Raban and his mother. Suggest that they begin by having her ask him why he is spending so much time down at the docks.

Four Point of View

Critical Reading

FOCUS

Jonathan Swift on satire:

"Satire is a sort of glass where beholders do generally discover everybody's face but their own."

BACKGROUND

A satire employs any number of devices that expose human or institutional vices and in which a corrective is either implied or directly proposed. Although satiric writing has been prevalent in European literature since Roman times, it found its greatest expression in the seventeenth and eighteenth centuries. Outstanding examples from the period include Molière's *Tartuffe,* Voltaire's *Candide,* and Jonathan Swift's *Gulliver's Travels.* The targets of satire are various. Hypocrisy, ambition, greed, piety, pride, materialism, and pretension are among the many weaknesses of the human character that have been pinpointed and ridiculed by the satirist's pen.

FOR DISCUSSION AND REFLECTION

➤ When did you first begin to suspect Waugh was making fun of the American tourists? (Answers will vary. Have students reread the opening to see how as they read a second time, many innocuous details seem satirical: "indomitable Americans," "like a completely unilluminated tube-railway station," and "Most of the Americans counted aloud with him.")

➤ What do you think is meant by the line "every one of the party in some way or another was bruised and upbraided by the thundering surf of education"? (On tours like this to historical monuments, guides often talk nonstop, offering tourists much more information that they could possibly process or store. As a result, the tourists feel "bruised" by the weight of the history they are being asked to carry and feel "upbraided" for being ignorant.)

➤ Why does Waugh decide not to deliver his imaginary speech to the American tourists? (He recalls that he had not been invited to join the group but had simply followed their tour. He was a "gate-crasher in this party.")

Writing

QUICK ASSESS

Do students' responses:

✓ identify words and phrases that support Waugh's purposes?

✓ demonstrate understanding of Waugh's writing?

Students are asked to quote words and phrases from the text that support Waugh's satiric purposes. To ensure that students know what they are looking for, make a list of the characteristics of these tourists that Waugh is satirizing.

READING AND WRITING EXTENSIONS

➤ Have students read passages from Evelyn Waugh's novel *A Handful of Dust,* which satirizes the superficiality and moral decay of the upper classes in England between World War I and World War II.

➤ Invite students to recall a moment of human folly that they have witnessed and then to try their hands at writing a satirical account of this sequence of events.

Five Establishing Points of Reference

Critical Reading

FOCUS

Isabel Fonseca has written that "Gypsies lie. They lie a lot—more often and more inventively than other people . . . . On the whole, lying is a cheerful affair. Embellishments are intended to give pleasure. People long to tell you what they imagine you want to hear. They want to amuse you; they want to amuse themselves; they want to show you a good time. This is beyond hospitality. This is art."

BACKGROUND

Bury Me Standing is both a history of Gypsies and a first-hand account of Isabel Fonseca's travels through Eastern Europe, living with Gypsy families and learning about their lives. Fonseca traces the Gypsies' exodus out of India 1,000 years ago and their astonishing history of persecution: enslaved by the princes of medieval Romania; massacred by the Nazis; forcibly assimilated by the communist regimes; and, most recently, evicted from their settlements by nationalist mobs throughout the new democracies of Eastern Europe. Fonseca's account paints a vivid portrait of the constraints and pleasures of Gypsy life.

FOR DISCUSSION AND REFLECTION

➤ What does Fonseca imply when she refers to the "institution of male laziness"? (In Gypsy culture the women do most of the work. The reference is clearly critical of this aspect of male Gypsy culture: "That the men did nothing came very quickly to seem not so much a privilege as a relegation to child status.")

➤ How would you describe Fonseca's attitude toward Viollca and Mirella? (Answers should include discussion about how she admires their industry and dedication to their task. Fonseca is frustrated by not being able to teach them to "bend from the knee." A part of her cannot help but want to ease their toil.)

➤ What evidence can you find regarding the girls' attitude toward Fonseca? (Their refusal to wake her suggests that they take little heed of such an irrational request. In response to Fonseca's pleas to "bend from the knee," they exchange "furtive, pitying giggles and glances." They think she is strange in her ways.)

Writing

QUICK ASSESS

Do students' lists:

✓ include several familiar and unfamiliar actions?

✓ explain the meanings of Fonseca's details?

Students are asked to explore the implications of the scene Fonseca has described. Help students to avoid the superficial analysis of this culture as simply primitive by asking students to think about the benefits of living in this kind of community.

READING AND WRITING EXTENSIONS

➤ Read students Emily Dickinson's poem "There is no frigate like a book" and encourage them to discuss how books carry readers to places they are unlikely ever to visit.

➤ Have students write what they imagine the two girls washing clothes think of Isabel Fonseca.

Unit Overview

The unifying topic of the poetry and nonfiction selections in this unit is the idea of home. As students explore the perspectives of writers such as Jessica Mitford and Virginia Woolf, they will understand the value of examining a variety of approaches to the same subject.

Literature Focus

	Lesson	Literature
1.	Idea Association	**Jessica Mitford,** from *Daughters and Rebels* (Nonfiction)
2.	Defining a Subject Through Objects	**Virginia Woolf,** from "Great Men's Houses" (Nonfiction)
3.	Developing Contrasts	**Virginia Woolf,** from "Great Men's Houses" (Nonfiction)
4.	Changing Perspectives	**Wole Soyinka,** "Telephone Conversation" (Poetry)
5.	Irony and Double Meanings	**Derek Walcott,** "The Virgins" (Poetry)

Reading Focus

1. Authors develop a subject with ideas and details that readers can relate to.
2. One way to develop a subject is to use objects that represent aspects of the subject.
3. Using contrasting details can highlight features of a topic more vividly than description alone.
4. Shifting perspectives on a subject reveals aspects of it that might otherwise be overlooked and enriches the reader's understanding of the topic.
5. Writers may use irony and words with double meanings to show the discrepancies between the ideal and the real forms of a subject.

Writing Focus

1. Write a brief sketch of your childhood home.
2. Use a description of a house to make inferences about its inhabitants.
3. Describe a home that you know, using details to convey the place's mood.
4. Continue the conversation of a poem.
5. Describe a real or imagined change to your home, using irony and double meanings to show the difference between the ideal and the real.

One Idea Association

C r i t i c a l   R e a d i n g

FOCUS

Jessica Mitford describing her childhood home:

"To me Swinbrook, where I spent most of my childhood, had aspects of a medieval fortress prison, from which quite early on I determined to escape."

BACKGROUND

Jessica Mitford was one of the famous and notorious daughters of Lord Redesdale, an eccentric British peer. He built Swinbrook House to satisfy the needs, as then seen, of a family with seven children. Mitford explains, "From the point of view of the inmates it was self-contained in the sense that it was neither necessary nor, generally, possible to leave the premises for any of the normal human pursuits. From the point of view of outsiders, entry, in the rather unlikely event that they might seek it, was an impossibility."

➤ Jessica and her five sisters were brought up at home, while Tom, their only brother, was sent to Eton. According to Mitford, "The dream of my childhood was to go to school. My mother taught us to read after which we graduated to the schoolroom, presided over by a succession of governesses, few of whom were able to put up for long with our relentless misbehavior."

FOR DISCUSSION AND REFLECTION

➤ Why do you think Mitford makes reference to idyllic, poetic images of the English countryside? (She uses them to contrast with her own bleak memories of winter giving way to "frosty spring" and merging into "chilly summer.")

➤ What does Mitford's repeated comment that "nothing ever, ever happened" suggest to you about the narrator? (Answers should include speculation that Mitford was most likely a child of great imagination and energy and that she felt stifled and bored in her childhood home.)

➤ How do you think you would like being educated at home? (Many responses are possible. Urge students to consider both the advantages and disadvantages.)

W r i t i n g

QUICK ASSESS

Do students' descriptions:

✓ include details of their childhood home?

✓ draw from Mitford's writing as a model?

Students are asked to write a brief description of their own childhood homes. Before they begin, discuss how their attitude toward this home will determine the details they choose.

READING AND WRITING EXTENSIONS

➤ Read students William Wordsworth's poem "I Wandered Lonely as a Cloud" and compare this poet's feelings toward daffodils with those of Jessica Mitford.

➤ Using Jessica Mitford's tone and attitude toward her childhood home as their evidence, have students write an essay analyzing Mitford's character.

Two Defining a Subject Through Objects

Critical Reading

FOCUS

Virginia Woolf wrote of the Carlyles that "One hour spent in 5 Cheyne Row will tell us more about them and their lives than we can learn from all the biographies."

BACKGROUND

Virginia Woolf is considered one of the great innovative novelists of the twentieth century. Many of her experimental techniques—such as the use of stream of consciousness and interior monologue—have been absorbed into the mainstream of fiction. Woolf was also a literary critic and journalist of distinction. In this excerpt from "Great Men's Houses," Virginia Woolf describes her visit to the house of Thomas Carlyle. She uses a combination of careful historical research and a highly tuned imagination to offer readers insight into the lives that were led within the walls of this great man's house. Detailing the hardships that conditions such as no running water or electricity place upon inhabitants, Woolf compares the mid-Victorian age house with a battleground. While the genius Carlyle "wrestled with his history," the women "fought against dirt and cold for cleanliness and warmth."

FOR DISCUSSION AND REFLECTION

➤ Do you agree or disagree with Woolf's thesis that one hour spent in a great man's house will tell you as much about the artist as a biography? (Many responses are possible. Encourage students to think about the different kinds of information the two sources provide in terms of insight into the lives of great men.)

➤ Why do you think Woolf believes that "half their quarrels might have been spared" had only the Carlyles had the comforts of modern living? (Woolf is suggesting that strife often springs from fatigue and resentment over tedious household chores.)

➤ How would you feel about living in a house such as that of the Carlyles? (Students' answers may include reference to the way modern conveniences dramatically ease the burden of running a household.)

Writing

QUICK ASSESS
Do students' descriptions:

✓ convey their impressions of the Carlyles?

✓ draw on Woolf's descriptive details?

Students are asked to write a description of the Carlyles based upon Woolf's description of their house. Choose one aspect of the house—for example, the lack of central heating in a cold climate—and together speculate on all the ways such a feature of a house affects inhabitants' lives.

READING AND WRITING EXTENSIONS

➤ Have students think again about the childhood home that they wrote about in the previous lesson. Ask them to describe how they think this house was perceived at the time by their mother or father.

➤ Ask students to read Phyllis Rose's account of Jane Welsh and Thomas Carlyle's life together from her book *Parallel Lives: Five Victorian Marriages.*

Three Developing Contrasts

Critical Reading

FOCUS

Virginia Woolf describes the effect Keats had upon his house as "the impression not of fever, but of that clarity and dignity which come from order and self-control."

BACKGROUND

John Keats began writing poetry at age eighteen and died from tuberculosis seven years later. Although his work reflects the powerful emotions typically found in romantic poetry, Keats did not share the social and political concerns of many of his contemporaries. He was obsessed with the qualities of beauty and with the private emotions of the individual.

➤ In this lesson, Virginia Woolf describes the house that Keats moved to in London following the death of his brother from tuberculosis in 1818. The poet immediately fell passionately in love with Fanny Brawne, his eighteen-year-old neighbor. Although they became engaged, ill health and poverty prevented the two from ever marrying. In the midst of this emotional turmoil, Keats produced his greatest works.

FOR DISCUSSION AND REFLECTION

➤ How does the house of John Keats differ from that of Thomas Carlyle? Why does Woolf say "it is always spring in Hampstead as it is always February in Cheyne Row"? (Answers should all reflect a careful reading of both passages. Have students support their opinions with lines from the text.)

➤ Do you think a person who had never read Keats' poetry would see all that Woolf has seen in the house and surroundings? (Read his "Ode to a Nightingale" to your class and then refer them to Woolf's line, "Here, for all the gaiety and serenity of neighborhood, the nightingale sang." Students may point out that knowledge of the poetry of John Keats is also essential for understanding Woolf's essay.)

➤ Woolf states that there is an "air of heroic equanimity about the house . . . ." What does this phrase suggest to you? (Many responses are possible, but they are likely to include the observation that despite Keats' internal passions, he lived in this house with a restraint that Woolf admires.)

Writing

QUICK ASSESS

Do students' descriptions:

✓ focus on a dwelling that they know?

✓ convey its mood and personality?

Students are asked to describe a dwelling that they know well, filling in details that convey the mood of the place. Have students make a list of possible houses they remember before choosing one that seems particularly charged with personality.

READING AND WRITING EXTENSIONS

➤ Read students "22 Hyde Park Gate," an essay by Woolf about the house in which she grew up. It was written to be read aloud to the Memoir Club, a group consisting of the members of the famous Bloomsbury Circle.

➤ John Keats was a master of the ode. Have students read "To Autumn" and then write an ode of their own in praise of a building or home that others might not consider worthy of elevated praise but that they find special.

Four Changing Perspectives

Critical Reading

FOCUS

Wole Soyinka explains that the African artist "has always functioned as the record of the mores and experience of his society."

BACKGROUND

A native of Nigeria, Wole Soyinka was awarded the 1986 Nobel Prize in Literature, becoming the first African to receive that honor. Soyinka believes that writers must become "a part of the machinery that will actually shape events." He often speaks out against political corruption and violations of human rights and was imprisoned for two years for sympathizing with Biafran rebels. Soyinka, best known as a playwright, currently lives in exile. In "Telephone Conversation," Soyinka satirizes British conceit, bigotry, prejudice, and the poet's own assimilation.

FOR DISCUSSION AND REFLECTION

➤ How do you think you would react if someone refused to rent you an apartment because of your race, gender, nationality, or religion? (Answers will vary, and some students may know of friends, neighbors, or family to whom this has happened. Have students compare their imagined response with that of the narrator in "Telephone Conversation.")

➤ How does the narrator feel about what has been revealed by this conversation? (The narrator is frustrated by the second-rate status he has been relegated to in this society and angry that he has accepted its prejudices as the status quo.)

➤ What message about discrimination do you think Soyinka is trying to convey? (Answers are likely to include reference to the way the speaker in this poem has been humiliated by the landlady's questions. Dominant cultures often treat minorities as inferiors and feel justified in their unfair treatment of them.)

Writing

QUICK ASSESS

Do students' writings:

✔ continue the conversation effectively?

✔ reflect the perspective of the speaker or the British woman?

Students are asked to write a continuation of the poem's conversation, taking on the perspective of either the speaker in the poem or the British woman. Before students write, have them role-play the situation with a partner.

READING AND WRITING EXTENSIONS

➤ Have students write about a time when they were discriminated against for being a teenager. How did they respond to the assumption that because of their youth they were therefore a problem?

➤ Have students read and discuss Derek Walcott's narrative poem *Midsummer*. In it, he describes his experience in England during the Brixton riots in 1981: "I was there to add some color to the British theater."

Five Irony and Double Meanings

Critical Reading

FOCUS

Derek Walcott describes himself as a "divided child." He is a Methodist living in a Catholic country, a black man with a white grandfather, a middle-class man living in the midst of lower-class poverty, a West Indian writing in the English tradition.

BACKGROUND

Derek Walcott, the first native Caribbean author to receive the Nobel Prize for Literature, has said that "I have felt from my boyhood that I had one function and that was somehow to articulate, not my own experience, but what I saw around me." His writing style combines English and West Indian features. In "The Virgins," Walcott uses irony to point out the inexhaustible greed of developers in the islands as well as the foolish naiveté of the islanders who are hungry for "the good life." In his Nobel acceptance speech, Walcott stated that "the process of poetry is one of excavation and of self-discovery." His work, as evidenced in the poem in Lesson Five, often voices opposition to the neglect of West Indian culture by the islands' British colonizers and by contemporary tourists.

FOR DISCUSSION AND REFLECTION

➤ How does Walcott use irony to describe what has happened to Frederiksted? (Students are likely to make references to the "life not lost to the American dream" and to "our new empire's civilized / exchange of cameras, watches, perfumes, brandies / for the good life." Islanders have exchanged their culture and native landscape for cheap trinkets.)

➤ Where in the poem does Walcott point out the damage that tourism has done? (Answers should include reference to the crime rate on the rise in "Frederiksted, / the first free port to die for tourism.")

➤ What is the double meaning of the title? (Walcott is making reference to the Virgin Islands and at the same time to the inexperience of the islanders compared to the experience of the American promoters of the islands.)

Writing

QUICK ASSESS

Do students' creations:

✓ describe a real or imagined change to their home?

✓ explain whether or not the change is for the better?

✓ use irony and double meanings?

Students are asked to use Walcott's poem as a model for a poem or paragraph of their own describing a real or imagined change to their home. Talk with students about the many possible forces that can operate upon a place to change it: weather, politics, economics, bad luck.

READING AND WRITING EXTENSIONS

➤ Derek Walcott is an accomplished painter as well as a writer. Bring in reproductions of his work and have students examine them to see if the paintings have themes similar to those expressed in his poems.

➤ Have students write an essay comparing Derek Walcott's and Wole Soyinka's poems in terms of their attitudes regarding cultures in conflict.

Unit Overview

This unit provides students with a variety of opportunities both to read closely and to write from models. As they read poems by Ted Hughes, Stephen Spender, A. E. Housman, and Henry Reed, students will create poems of their own, including a spinoff poem, an emulation, and an ode.

Literature Focus

	Lesson	Literature
1.	Point of View	**Ted Hughes,** "Hawk Roosting" (Poetry)
2.	Spinoff Modeling	**Stephen Spender,** "I Think Continually of Those" (Poetry)
3.	Modeling an Ode	**A. E. Housman,** "To an Athlete Dying Young" (Poetry)
4.	Modeling Voice	**Henry Reed,** "Naming of Parts" from *Lessons of the War* (Poetry)
5.	Modeling Situation	

Reading Focus

1. Understanding a poem through modeling provides insight into points of view other than your own.
2. Poets often spin off a poem from the inspiration of another poet's lines. It is a method of practice and interpretation.
3. The ode is a classical form still widely used by poets for both serious and trivial subjects.
4. Modeling the voice or voices of the narrator of a poem requires a close reading of the original.
5. In modeling, you choose an important element of the original scenario—in this case the prosaic and reflective voices—and write your own poem.

Writing Focus

1. Compose a poem in which the speaker is an animal.
2. Blend lines from Spender's poem with your own to create a spinoff poem.
3. Write an ode.
4. Write an emulation.
5. Write a poem that includes both inner and outer voices.

One Point of View

Critical Reading

FOCUS

Ted Hughes's poetry is noted for its violence of feeling, powerful imagery, and metrical virtuosity.

BACKGROUND

On a literal level, "Hawk Roosting" is a portrait of a magnificently egocentric creature unaware of any of his own limitations. The hawk believes that "the whole of Creation" has culminated in his superior position and that his own physical characteristics allow him to make fullest use of the rest of nature. The details in the hawk's monologue are precise and wholly focused on his view of himself as the center of the universe: "And the earth's face upward for my inspection." His flight causes the earth to revolve. The limited perspective creates the poem's irony. Readers know much more about the hawk than the hawk does himself. We know he is mortal, that his mastery of his environment is circumstantial, and that he is not the highest creature in existence. Students may need help with the definition of *sophistry* as clever and subtle but perhaps misleading reasoning.

FOR DISCUSSION AND REFLECTION

➤ How would you characterize the personality of the speaker in this poem? (Students are likely to mention the hawk's megalomania. He is convinced that the world revolves around him: "I sit in the top of the wood . . . .")

➤ What do you think the hawk means when he says "There is no sophistry in my body: / My manners are tearing off heads—"? (Answers should point to the hawk's view that he has no need to engage in explanations or arguments because his business is killing. He answers to no one for his actions.)

➤ Have you ever known anyone who resembles the hawk in his attitude toward the world around him? (Have students explain their answers.)

Writing

QUICK ASSESS

Do students' poems:

✓ have an animal as the speaker?

✓ consist of three or more stanzas?

✓ use words effectively?

Students are asked to write a poem from the point of view of another animal. Suggest to students that they give their narrators an attitude—meek, bold, fearful, tyrannical—to match the physical characteristics.

READING AND WRITING EXTENSIONS

➤ Ask students to reflect on one of the photographs in the *Daybook*. Have them describe the scene from the point of view of the photographer or from a person shown in the picture.

➤ Have students write an interior monologue for a bird-watcher observing this hawk from a distance. How will this person's point of view be different from that of the hawk?

Two Spinoff Modeling

Critical Reading

FOCUS

Stephen Spender writes that those who are truly great leave "the vivid air signed with their honor."

BACKGROUND

Stephen Spender was one of the leading left-wing poets in the 1930s. Much of Spender's poetry deals with his own emotional reactions as he contemplates poverty, suffering, and injustice or visualizes a better life in a socialist state. He was deeply interested in the public and social duty of a writer. In "I Think Continually of Those," Spender illustrates the characteristics of great men and women and celebrates their passion. Many of the poem's images point to these individuals' abilities to remain concentrated upon their goal. In the final stanza, Spender describes how the world honors the truly great: "these names are fêted by the waving grass, / And by the streamers of white cloud, / And whispers of wind in the listening sky."

FOR DISCUSSION AND REFLECTION

➤ What do you think might cause someone to "think continually of those who were truly great"? (Students will have many ideas, but they should speculate that the speaker may be measuring himself against those great men and women.)

➤ How do you interpret the statement that what is precious is "Never to allow gradually the traffic to smother / With noise and fog the flowering of the spirit"? (As they answer, students may want to discuss how we, like the truly great, must not allow ourselves to be distracted or dismayed by everyday matters but instead must be able to keep focused on the life within and the work to be done.)

➤ If someone said to you that you wore at your heart "the fire's center," what do you think they would be suggesting about your personality? (It would likely mean that you cared passionately about issues and made them the focus of your life.)

Writing

QUICK ASSESS

Do students' poems:

✔ intermix their own lines with those from Spender's poem?

✔ begin with Spender's first line?

✔ include two or three stanzas?

Students are asked to write a poem in which they include Stephen Spender's first line as their own. Suggest that students begin by highlighting the other lines and phrases from "I Think Continually of Those" that they plan to use in their poem.

READING AND WRITING EXTENSIONS

➤ Have students write a letter to the school newspaper nominating an unsung hero who should be celebrated with a new school holiday.

➤ Read to students Spender's poem "Icarus" and discuss together the political subtext he has given to the myth.

Three Modeling an Ode

Critical Reading

FOCUS

An ode is a lyric poem of exalted emotion, devoted to the praise or celebration of its subject.

BACKGROUND

A. E. Housman was a classical scholar who became famous from a single volume of poetry, *A Shropshire Lad* (1896). The poems were set against a background of the English countryside and are marked by irony and a melancholy sense of the transitory nature of youth and love. Their tone has been ascribed to the poet's disappointment at his mediocre performance in his final examinations at Oxford University and to his strong feelings for a college friend, Moses Jackson, referred to in the poems as Terence. In "To an Athlete Dying Young," the speaker is a fellow townsman of the dead athlete. The young man died within months of winning the annual race for his town. After his victory in the race, the townspeople had "chaired" him, borne him in triumph on their shoulders. Now, less than a year later, they bring him home again. This time "home" is a metaphor for the grave. The "road all runners come" is death, and the youth is being borne "Shoulder-high" in his coffin.

FOR DISCUSSION AND REFLECTION

➤ How does the rhyme and rhythm of this poem affect you as a reader? (Possible responses may include liking the song-like qualities that rhyme and rhythm create in a poem.)

➤ Why is the message of the third stanza likely to shock readers? (Answers will vary. Most people would consider the death of a young athlete an occasion for sadness, but the speaker congratulates the boy for dying while everyone is still singing his praises.)

➤ Can you discern the mythological reference in the final stanza? (In Book 11 of the *Odyssey*, Odysseus visits the underworld and is surrounded by shades of the "strengthless dead," many of whom were once heroes.)

Writing

QUICK ASSESS

Do students' odes:

✓ address the subject directly?

✓ follow the traditional rhythm and rhyme patterns?

Students are asked to write an ode of their own. In order to help them think about a subject for their poems, bring in odes by Keats, Shelley, Burns, and others for students to read.

READING AND WRITING EXTENSIONS

➤ The Chilean poet Pablo Neruda has written a series of odes to common things. They break many of the customs of traditional ode-writing in their short lines, lack of rhyme, and extensive length, but they remain true to the spirit of traditional odes in that they sing the praises of spoons, onions, oranges, socks, and other familiar objects. Read students examples of Neruda's modern odes.

➤ Invite students to imagine that an athlete they admire has unexpectedly died. Have them write a diary entry for themselves reflecting upon the person's achievements and whether the sport will be different without him or her.

Four Modeling Voice

Critical Reading

FOCUS

In "Naming of Parts," the trainees and the gardens represent a series of opposites: death versus life, the mechanical versus the natural, regimentation versus freedom, tedium versus joy.

BACKGROUND

In Henry Reed's poem "Naming of Parts," a sergeant is giving instructions to a group of army trainees. There are two voices in the poem, but the dialogue is conducted within the mind of one person, that of a sensitive recruit. The first three or so lines of all but the last stanza are the spoken words of the sergeant as heard by the recruit. The last lines of these stanzas, and the whole of the final stanza, are the unspoken thoughts of the recruit. His unspoken thoughts furnish a comment on the instruction he receives.

➤ Help students to understand that the meaning of the poem grows out of the ironic contrast between the trainees and the gardens. The gardens represent the natural, the free, the graceful, the beautiful—everything that is missing from the lives of the soldiers. Through this ironic juxtaposition, the poet comments on the kind of life imposed by war.

FOR DISCUSSION AND REFLECTION

➤ Why do you think Henry Reed chose to repeat certain phrases through the poem? (Students may comment on how the same words in different mouths can take on opposite meanings—for example, "easing the Spring."

➤ How do the language and rhythm of the poem support its central contrast? (The words of the sergeant are pedestrian, and their rhythm is like prose, frequently faltering and clumsy. The lines about the gardens are full of rich imagery and flowing rhythm. The abrupt change in rhythm is particularly striking in the middle of line 17.)

➤ What statement about war does the poem make? (One answer is that by contrasting natural life with instruction in killing, the poem makes a powerful anti-war statement.)

Writing

QUICK ASSESS

Do students' emulations:

✓ combine a prosaic and a reflective voice?

✓ imitate Reed's double meanings?

Students are asked to imitate the double meanings of Reed's lines. This poem is heavy with double meanings that can open up further discussion of the poem's theme.

READING AND WRITING EXTENSIONS

➤ Keith Douglass wrote of World War I poetry that "The behavior of the living and the appearance of the dead were so accurately described by the poets of the Great War that every day on the battlefields of the western desert their poems are illustrated." Ask students to think about how that statement might apply to Reed's poems or other war poetry that they know.

➤ Have students take on the persona of the recruit in "Naming of Parts" and write a letter home to his younger brother who is keen on the idea of joining the army.

Five Modeling Situation

Critical Reading

FOCUS

Laurence Perrine, author of *Sound and Sense*, wrote that "discussions will serve their purpose if they provoke a more careful scrutiny of the poems."

BACKGROUND

In *The Art of Fiction*, John Gardner wrote that "Art depends heavily on feeling, intuition, taste. It is feeling, not some rule, that tells the abstract painter to put his yellow here, not there, and may later tell him that it should have been brown or purple or pea-green. It's feeling that gives the writer the rhythms of his sentences, the pattern of rise and fall in his episodes so that dialogue goes on only so long before a shift to description or some physical action. The great writer has an instinct for these things. And his instinct touches every thread of his fabric, even the murkiest fringes of symbolic structure."

FOR DISCUSSION AND REFLECTION

➤ Read students the quotation from John Gardner and ask them to apply what he has said to the poems they have read in this unit. How have Ted Hughes, Stephen Spender, A. E. Housman, and Henry Reed demonstrated their instinct for language and rhythm? (Urge students to support their opinions with evidence from the poems.)

➤ What could you tell about the character of Reed's recruit from the nature of his inner musings? (Students may refer to his sensitivity, his keen observations, his clever way of juxtaposing events outside himself with inner feelings.)

➤ What have you been thinking about as the class read and discussed these poems? Have you experienced an inner and outer voice? (The purpose of this question is to help students see that most people have two conversations going on at once: one with the outer world, another with themselves.)

Writing

QUICK ASSESS

Do students' poems:

✓ include both inner and outer voices?

✓ describe a scenario with details?

Students are asked to create a scenario in which a speaker is doing something that requires his or her outward attention while inwardly thinking about something else. Before they begin to write, have students share examples of times when this has happened to them.

READING AND WRITING EXTENSIONS

➤ Read students A. E. Housman's "Is My Team Plowing," a poetic conversation in two voices, one dead and one alive. Ask students to compare Housman's use of contrasting speakers with that of Henry Reed.

➤ Have students write an interpretive essay explaining the use of inner and outer voices in "Naming of Parts."

Unit Overview

In this unit, as students read Dylan Thomas' "Fern Hill" and excerpts from James Joyce's *A Portrait of the Artist as a Young Man*, they will explore how writers draw on personal memories in their works. Students will write original poems and scenes based on their own childhoood memories.

Literature Focus

	Lesson	Literature
1.	Images of Childhood	**Dylan Thomas,** "Fern Hill" (Poetry)
2.	Childhood Memory	
3.	The Language of Memory	**James Joyce,** from *A Portrait of the Artist as a Young Man* (Fiction)
4.	Stream of Consciousness	**James Joyce,** from *A Portrait of the Artist as a Young Man* (Fiction)
5.	Daydreaming and Epiphanies	**James Joyce,** from *A Portrait of the Artist as a Young Man* (Fiction)

Reading Focus

1. Noticing the kind of images a writer uses enables you to imagine the scenes for yourself as you read.
2. Crafting memories into a poem requires careful attention to both images and form.
3. Understanding the language of memory requires readers to be open to the author's style.
4. Through stream-of-consciousness writing, authors can reveal personality, recurrent thoughts, and character.
5. An epiphany often marks an important turning point or realization in a novel. Such a moment ususally occurs when a completely ordinary event takes on special significance.

Writing Focus

1. Explain why certain images in a poem are effective.
2. Write a poem about a childhood place.
3. Use sensory details to write a scene from your early childhood.
4. Describe a character from different perspectives.
5. Write an account of an epiphany you have experienced.

One Images of Childhood

Critical Reading

FOCUS

Dylan Thomas laments that "time allows / In all his tuneful turning so few and such morning songs / Before the children green and golden / Follow him out of grace."

BACKGROUND

In "Fern Hill," Dylan Thomas recreates the delight, the wonder, the long and carefree rapture of boyhood summers spent on a farm in Wales. The reader shares in his pleasure in the barns and fields and orchards, in the farmhouse itself, in the animals, in afternoon and night and morning. In the fourth stanza, the poet compares this boyhood experience to the experience of Adam and Eve in Eden. Like theirs, its chief characteristics were joy and innocence and a feeling of timelessness. Like theirs, his experience came at the beginning of life and, like them, he felt it would last forever. But the theme of the poem is the transience of youthful joy and carefree innocence.

FOR DISCUSSION AND REFLECTION

➤ Who is the speaker in this poem and why does he speak in the past tense? (The speaker is an adult Dylan Thomas reflecting upon his joyous and carefree youth.)

➤ How do you interpret the phrase "lamb white days"? What shades of meaning would have been lost if Thomas had used "snow white" instead? (Answers should include that in Wales, where this poem occurs, lambs are common, while snow is not. *Lamb* also carries the connotation of innocence that is key to this poem's theme.)

➤ What familiar sayings about time has Thomas used? How has he lent a freshness to these sayings? (Many responses are possible. Students should point to the way slight alterations of a phrase cause readers to see new meanings in a line. Point students to lines 4–5, lines 13–14, lines 41–45, line 50, and lines 53–54.)

Writing

QUICK ASSESS

Do students' writings:

✓ identify several particular images?

✓ explain why certain images evoked scenes of childhood so powerfully?

Students are asked to describe the images which are most powerful in evoking scenes from Thomas' childhood. Discuss with students how a reader's familiarity with a rural setting might influence the choice of imagery.

READING AND WRITING EXTENSIONS

➤ Find a copy of Dylan Thomas' reading of this poem in your local library and play it for the class. His voice is as "golden" as his poetry.

➤ Have students write about a "green and golden" moment from their own childhood. Encourage them to employ a range of images the way Thomas has in "Fern Hill."

Two Childhood Memory

Critical Reading

FOCUS

From "The Force that through the Green Fuse Drives the Flower," by Dylan Thomas:

"The lips of time leech to the fountain head; / Love drips and gathers, but the fallen blood / Shall calm her sores. / And I am dumb to tell a weather's wind / How time has ticked a heaven round the stars."

BACKGROUND

One of the most common features of storytelling is the presence of a protagonist and an antagonist. In "Fern Hill," the boy is the protagonist and time is the antagonist. Though unseen and unfelt by the child, the adult looking back understands this antagonist clearly. The boy, "happy as the grass was green," feels that these summers will last forever. But, inexorably, in its alternation of afternoon and night and morning, Time is carrying him out of the enchanted realm, "out of grace," toward age and death. The boy who is "prince of the apple towns" and who feels himself master of all he surveys is, in fact, a slave held by "Time" in "chains."

FOR DISCUSSION AND REFLECTION

➤ How does time lead "the children green and golden" out of grace? (Be sure that students understand the connotations of *grace* and can apply it to the boy's childhood idyll. Like a Pied Piper, "in all his tuneful turning," Time lures children out of the garden of innocent youth into the world of experience.)

➤ Poetry is for both the ear and the eye. Without actually rereading the poem, have students consider the appearance of the poem. What does your eye tell you about the pattern and shape of the stanzas? (Answers should suggest the organic nature of the poem. It seems alive and changeable.)

➤ Reread the poem aloud, focusing on the sound of the words. What does your ear tell you about this poem that your eye could not? (There is a strong musical quality to the poem; Dylan Thomas invites readers to follow.)

Writing

QUICK ASSESS
Do students' poems:

✔ describe a place from their childhood?

✔ create a vivid impression for readers?

Students are asked to write a poem about a place from their childhoods that they remember vividly. Remind students of the various forms of poetry that they might choose as a structure for their poem. Encourage them to chose a form that reinforces the theme that they want to communicate.

READING AND WRITING EXTENSIONS

➤ Read students Robert Frost's "Nothing Gold Can Stay" and discuss together his metaphorical use of gold: "Nature's first green is gold."

➤ Ask students to construct a found poem, using only words from "Fern Hill." Suggest that they focus on either color, time, or childhood.

Three The Language of Memory

Critical Reading

FOCUS

Joyce's epigraph for *A Portrait of the Artist as a Young Man* is taken from a description of Daedalus in Ovid's *Metamorphoses* and reads, "And he applies his mind to unknown arts."

BACKGROUND

James Joyce is arguably the most influential modern writer. Though his novel *Ulysses* has evoked more critical discussion, *A Portrait of the Artist as a Young Man* is Joyce's most widely read work. Despite its surface challenges, young people respond to the book's convincing portrayal of a sensitive youth harrowed by religious and sexual guilt and transfigured by an idea of beauty. This excerpt takes the reader into the world of a four-year-old Stephen Dedalus, a world in which the line between stories and real life is indistinct.

FOR DISCUSSION AND REFLECTION

➤ How do you interpret the opening line, "Once upon a time and a very good time it was . . . ."? (Answers might include that Joyce uses the most traditional of story starters as a way to prepare readers for the archetypal qualities of the story he is about to tell. The line also offers readers a clue to the narrator's attitude toward the events he is about to describe.)

➤ Why do you think Joyce included childhood rhymes in this part of the novel? (These songs and verses run through young Stephen's mind constantly. Joyce is describing the internal landscape of someone who goes on to become an artist.)

➤ Why do you think adults threaten children with horrible consequences—"the eagles will come and pull out his eyes"—for not behaving? (Among possible responses are threats that are part of most children's growing up. Students should recognize that one reason for these dire predictions is the need of adults to impress upon the child the importance of behaving well. The someday-to-be artist turns the threats into verse.)

Writing

QUICK ASSESS

Do students' scenes:

✔ recreate a moment from their own childhood?

✔ include sensory details?

Students are asked to recreate a moment from their own childhoods. Before they begin to write, have students think about this memory from a time when they were very small.

READING AND WRITING EXTENSIONS

➤ Have students rewrite the incident from their own childhoods from the point of view of an adult who either was present or heard about what happened.

➤ Read students examples of nursery rhymes and ask them to compare these with the rhymes Joyce has incorporated into this excerpt from *A Portrait of the Artist as a Young Man*.

Four Stream of Consciousness

Critical Reading

FOCUS

J.C. Squire, an early reviewer of *A Portrait of the Artist as a Young Man*, wrote that Joyce's portrayal of speech "is as close to the dialogue of life as anything I have ever come across."

BACKGROUND

When he was six years old, James Joyce was sent away to boarding school at Clongowes Wood College. Run by Jesuits, Clongowes was perhaps the best preparatory school in Ireland. Despite the repressive picture he paints of the school in *A Portrait of the Artist as a Young Man*, Joyce spoke warmly of his experience there. Joyce was a good student at Clongowes, and in some ways he never abandoned the habits of thought with which the Jesuits inculcated him.

➤ In this excerpt from his schooldays, Stephen recounts the confusion he felt when no answer he offered was correct, and he tells of the discomfort of being thrown into a ditch. The two events merge into one another, as the artist reflects on love and cruelty. Joyce bares a cross section of the little boy's mind as it darts back and forth between memories of home and his first school experiences.

FOR DISCUSSION AND REFLECTION

➤ What evidence can you find in this excerpt that points to Stephen's not being one of the boys? (Many responses are possible. Stephen is afraid and only pretends to be playing in order to keep out of trouble. He feels small, weak, and inadequate.)

➤ What does the fact that Stephen's thoughts alternate between home and school suggest to you? (The boy is probably homesick and missing his mother.)

➤ There was a student named Wells at Clongowes in Joyce's time, and he may have been the boy who pushed young James Joyce into the square ditch. If you were writing a novel, why might you use the names of actual people? (Some students are likely to see this as a way of exacting revenge.)

Writing

QUICK ASSESS

Do students' descriptions:

✔ reflect details from the story?

✔ express how other people would see Stephen?

Students are asked to write a series of short descriptions of Stephen as other people in the story see him. Encourage students to speculate rather than search for correct answers. Good readers make tentative assumptions about relationships between characters that they later often revise.

READING AND WRITING EXTENSIONS

➤ Have students write about a time when they felt that whatever answer they gave to another person was going to be wrong.

➤ Ask students to research the mythological story of Daedalus and draw connections between Daedalus and Icarus and Stephen Dedalus. Discuss together which qualities of the character Joyce might choose to explore in the character of Stephen.

Five Daydreaming and Epiphanies

Critical Reading

FOCUS

In the final lines of *A Portrait of the Artist as a Young Man*, Stephen Dedalus writes in his journal, "I go to encounter for the millionth time the reality of experience and to forge in the smithy of my soul the uncreated conscience of my race."

BACKGROUND

A Portrait of the Artist as a Young Man is often read as an autobiography, and, in fact, many of the incidents in it come from Joyce's youth. But it would be a mistake to assume that James Joyce was exactly like his sober hero, Stephen Dedalus. Joyce's younger brother called it "a lying autobiography and a raking satire." Joyce transformed autobiography into fiction by selecting, sifting, and reconstructing scenes from his own life to create a portrait of Stephen Dedalus, a sensitive and serious young boy who gradually comes to define himself as an artist.

FOR DISCUSSION AND REFLECTION

➤ Based upon what you read in this excerpt, how would you characterize Stephen as a student? (Students should mention Stephen's habit of using the subject of a lesson as a springboard for his own mental expeditions. From a very early age, he seems to care about big ideas and poetry.)

➤ Ask students what they understand of the word *epiphany*. (*Epiphany* comes from the Greek for "a manifestation; a showing forth." It was familiar to Joyce from the Christian festival of Epiphany, which commemorates the manifestation of Christ to the Magi on Twelfth Night. Joyce used the term to refer to a moment of revelation in which a main character and/or the reader has a sudden insight into the true nature of a person, situation, idea, or life.)

➤ What epiphany does Stephen seem to experience? (Possible responses include the thought that whatever men might choose to call God remains unchanged and unchangeable.)

Writing

QUICK ASSESS

Do students' writings:

✓ focus on an epiphany of their own?

✓ avoid explaining the moment's significance?

✓ jump right into the scene?

Students are asked to write an account of an epiphany they have experienced. In order to avoid the roadblock of students saying that they have never experienced one, brainstorm a long list of moments when students have felt a sense of "Aha!" in their lives.

READING AND WRITING EXTENSIONS

➤ Literature is full of famous daydreamers. Read to students from Huckleberry Finn's musings on the raft in Chapter IX of Mark Twain's *Huckleberry Finn*. As students listen to what Huck says about his and Jim's place in the universe, ask them to compare these ideas with Stephen Dedalus's view.

➤ Have students chart their own personal geography, beginning with their name and continuing through at least seven steps to "The Universe."

Unit Overview

William Butler Yeats was one of the most significant writers of the twentieth century. In this unit, as students explore several of his poems and his description of the artistic process, they will study Yeats' use of imagery, symbolism, and meter and learn about his views of life and art.

Literature Focus

	Lesson	Literature
1.	Image and Symbol	"The Wild Swans at Coole" (Poetry)
2.	The Dramatic Lyric	"Coole Park, 1929" (Poetry)
3.	Lines That Transcend Time	"The Second Coming" (Poetry)
4.	Poem as Autobiography	"What Then?" (Poetry)
5.	The Artistic Process	from the Introduction to *The Oxford Book of Modern Verse* (Nonfiction)

Reading Focus

1. An image becomes a symbol when it means both what it actually is and stands for something else as well. Writers often use recurrent symbols throughout their work.

2. In a dramatic lyric, the poet explores ideas and images through the natural rhythms of the language of speech.

3. Recognizing and understanding great lines of poetry that have become part of our heritage is one of the benefits of reading widely.

4. In autobiographical poems, the poet reveals glimpses of ideas about the meaning of life.

5. A writer's views about art provide insight into the art itself.

Writing Focus

1. Explain a poem's symbolism.
2. Describe the changing meaning of a poem's imagery.
3. Write about the relevance of a poem today.
4. Write a poem inspired by Yeats' "What Then?"
5. Comment on Yeats' view of the artistic process.

One Image and Symbol

Critical Reading

FOCUS

Thomas Arp described the swans in "The Wild Swans at Coole" as "genuinely mysterious, for the poem has not penetrated their mysteries, but seen in them parallels and contrasts to the human condition."

BACKGROUND

William Butler Yeats' theory and practice of writing both point to the need to read any poem of his in the context of the rest of his poetry and in the context of his life. Given the dictates of time as well as the nature of most high school students, this is rarely possible to achieve. The goal of this unit is to provide students with background material to scaffold their reading and to help them to recognize that there is much more in the poem. One hopes that the love for Yeats' poetry that this unit sparks will send students back again and again to his work.

➤ "The Wild Swans at Coole" is a meditation on nature and the passage of time that alters the human observer but leaves nature essentially unchanged. The elegiac tone is established in the first stanza with references to autumn, dryness, twilight, and stillness. Yeats contrasts these images with images of beauty, demonstrating his inability to understand the swans with the declaration that "But now they drift on the still water, / Mysterious, beautiful . . . ."

FOR DISCUSSION AND REFLECTION

➤ Why do you think the speaker is so careful about counting the swans and the number of summers he has been coming to Coole? (Many responses are possible but should include discussion of the human desire to figure things out and pin them down to statistical truths while nature is reluctant to be measured with accuracy.)

➤ How are the swans personified? (Their wings beat like bells, they are lovers, the water is "Companionable," they are "Unwearied," their hearts do not grow old.)

➤ Yeats often concluded his poems with rhetorical questions. How do you interpret the final lines? (Answers will vary, but since the swans represent to the speaker the continuity and permanence of the natural world, any awakening that discovers them gone will be an awakening out of nature, into death.)

Writing

QUICK ASSESS

Do students' responses:

✓ reflect a thoughtful reading of the poem?

✓ explain what the swans meant to Yeats?

Students are asked to write about what they think the swans meant to Yeats. Before they begin, write *swan* on the board and cluster around it all the denotations and connotations of the word.

READING AND WRITING EXTENSIONS

➤ Invite students to write a one-stanza poem about how the passage of time has changed their perception of a person or place. Suggest that they use the rhyme and structure of the first stanza of "The Wild Swans at Coole" as a model.

➤ Ask students to figure out how many times they have gone to a place they love and then write about how a recurring image from that place has come to have symbolic meaning for them.

Two The Dramatic Lyric

Critical Reading

FOCUS

In an early poem, Yeats wrote, "A line will take us hours maybe, / Yet if it does not seem a moment's thought, / Our stitching and unstitching has been naught."

BACKGROUND

Yeats wrote only four or five lines of poetry a day throughout most of his life. His idea of craft was one of technique achieved through long practice and long experiment. The result is a poem that sounds like casual speech. "Coole Park, 1929" is a dramatic lyric poem in which a clearly defined speaker—Yeats himself—explores the idea of how Lady Gregory's hospitality to writers has been a lasting legacy to art.

FOR DISCUSSION AND REFLECTION

➤ What is there about Coole Park that makes it such an ideal setting for writers? (Students should point to the description of a beautiful place in which imagination could be given full rein: "Great works constructed there in nature's spite . . . .")

➤ In what way are the artists Yeats mentions like swallows? (Many answers are possible, but they should include discussion of how the birds come to Coole Park, depart at summer's end, but always return. Through the influence of "a woman's powerful character," for a time, they moved in unison intellectually.)

➤ How do you interpret Yeats' instructions to travelers, scholars, and poets in his final stanza? (Yeats reminds all those who have been beneficiaries of Lady Gregory's hospitality to dedicate "A moment's memory to that laurelled head." He wants them to honor the person who has made so much art possible.)

Writing

QUICK ASSESS

Do students' responses:

✓ explain the symbolic meanings of the swallows?

✓ discuss how the symbolism changes from stanza one to stanza three?

Students are asked to write about how the meaning of the swallow image changes from stanza one to stanza three. Some students may need background information on the physical characteristics and habits of this bird in order to write with any specificity about Yeats' use of the swallow as a symbol.

READING AND WRITING EXTENSIONS

➤ Invite students to research the life of William Butler Yeats. Have them share with the class interesting facts they find.

➤ Ask students to describe a place where they might go to pursue their own most important dreams. Have students identify their own goal and then imagine the particular location where they could best pursue that goal.

Three Lines That Transcend Time

Critical Reading

FOCUS

Helen Vendler wrote that "Yeats approves intellectually, if not emotionally, of the Second Coming. The Beast is a world-restorer."

BACKGROUND

In 1919, the year this poem was published, Ireland was in the midst of a bloody civil war; World War I had only recently ended; and Russia was engaged in civil war following its revolution of 1917. All these events portended for Yeats the approaching end of the Christian era, the historical cycle begun almost two thousand years earlier with the birth of Christ. In Yeats' historical theory, the transition from one historical era to another is always marked by an epoch of violence and disorder. The "Second Coming" refers both to the return of Christ, as foretold in the book of Matthew, and to the coming of the Antichrist, the beast of the Apocalypse, described in the Book of Revelation. Yeats foresaw a time of chaos and destruction as the spiral begins to form a new center.

➤ *Spiritus Mundi* is Latin for "spirit of the world." In this poem, it refers to what Carl Jung called the collective unconscious or the vast body of knowledge that is available to all human beings if they know how to tap into it.

FOR DISCUSSION AND REFLECTION

➤ How would you characterize Yeats' impression of current conditions in the world? (Students should mention a world out of control. The images are terrifying.)

➤ Though the first two lines of the second stanza seem to offer hope—"Surely some revelation is at hand . . ."—what impression are you left with at the end of the poem? (Our expectation that the poem would concern the Second Coming of Christ is shattered by the last two lines of the poem. It is the coming of the Antichrist that is prophesied.)

➤ If you were to choose a line from this poem for the title of a novel you may one day write, which would you choose? (Have students explain how their choices would match the message of their story.)

Writing

QUICK ASSESS

Do students' responses:

✓ explain the relevance of this poem today?

✓ refer to specific lines?

Students are asked to write about the relevance of this poem. Have students discuss the ways in which they see things falling apart in our society. Why does the center seem to be unable to hold in a twentieth-century world?

READING AND WRITING EXTENSIONS

➤ Joan Didion titled her collection of essays about the 1960s *Slouching Towards Bethlehem*. Have groups of students read selections from it and speculate on why this phrase applies to these essays.

➤ Many contemporary films recreate scenes of near-total world destruction. Have students choose an apocalyptic moment from the screen and explain why they did or didn't find this rendering believable.

Four Poem as Autobiography

Critical Reading

After receiving a medal—symbolizing the Nobel Prize—depicting a young man listening to a Muse, Yeats wrote, "I was good-looking once like that young man, but my unpractised verse was full of infirmity, my Muse old as it were, and now I am old and rheumatic and nothing to look at, but my Muse is young."

BACKGROUND

In 1917, when he was fifty-two, Yeats began to concern himself with the problem of the older poet. Students may consider fifty-two old age and need to be reminded that this was a man in his prime considering his future. He wrote, "A poet, when he is growing old, will ask himself if he cannot keep his mask and his vision, without new bitterness, new disappointment. Could he if he would, copy Landor who lived loving and hating, ridiculous and unconquered, into extreme old age, all lost but the favor of his muses. Surely, he may think, now that I have found vision and mask I need not suffer any longer. Then he will remember Wordsworth, withering into eighty years, honored and empty-witted, and climb to some waste room, and find, forgotten there by youth, some bitter crust."

FOR DISCUSSION AND REFLECTION

➤ How do you interpret the question "'What then?'" as posed at the end of the first stanza? (Students are likely to comment that though full of promise and working hard at his craft, the poet worries about what he should put his mind to next.)

➤ Based upon evidence from the poem, what do you think Yeats' personal and professional life was like? (He experienced success as a poet and dramatist and earned enough money from his writing to support himself and his family. He had many companions; "Poets and Wits about him drew.")

➤ Why do you think the ghost sang more loudly in the final stanza? (Many responses are possible, but students should see that even with all the accomplishments that talent and hard work had brought him Yeats continues to ponder what will come next; what happens to a man when "The work is done"?)

Writing

QUICK ASSESS

Do students' poems:

✓ consist of three stanzas?

✓ include a refrain?

✓ use Yeats' opening in their beginnings?

Students are asked to write a poem about their own lives using Yeats' opening as a starting point. Before they begin to write, brainstorm a number of possible short refrains on the board.

READING AND WRITING EXTENSIONS

➤ Ask students to write a short answer for each time the ghost of Plato asks "'What then?'"

➤ Have students read W. H. Auden's poem "In Memory of W. B. Yeats" (pages 182, 184, 185) and discuss how Auden's feelings about Yeats compare with their own.

Five The Artistic Process

Critical Reading

FOCUS

Yeats on his writing:

"If I can be sincere and make my language natural, and without becoming discursive like a novelist, and so indiscreet and prosaic, I shall, if good or bad luck make my life interesting, be a great poet; for it will not longer be a question of literature at all."

BACKGROUND

In a 1938 issue of *The Atlantic Monthly*, poet Louise Bogan wrote of Yeats: "Where so much of the spirit of art had to be revivified, so many of its forms repaired, and so tight a mould of fanaticism broken, a man was needed who had in himself some of the qualities of the fanatic—a man who was, above all else, an artist, capable of making an occasional compromise with a human being, but incapable of making one with the informing essence of his art. New light and air had to be let into the closed minds and imaginations of a people made suspicious and hysterically provincial through persecution and disaster. Not only insight and imagination, but ruthlessness, fervor, disinterestedness, and a capacity for decision and action, were required."

FOR DISCUSSION AND REFLECTION

➤ What do you think Yeats means when he says that the "progress of an artist is a continual self-sacrifice . . ."? (Students may at first refer to the starving artist cliché. Help them to see that this is not what Yeats is talking about in terms of "self-sacrifice," but rather the separation of the "man who suffers" from the "man who creates.")

➤ How would you put Yeats' comparison of the mind of the poet with a shred of platinum into your own words? (Accept all reasonable responses. This is a wonderful opportunity for the scientists in the classroom to shine.)

➤ Does Yeats' explanation of what the creation of art requires make you want to be an artist, make you recoil at the thought of such a life, or have new respect for artists? (There is no one correct answer here. Encourage students to explore all three positions.)

Writing

QUICK ASSESS

Do students' explanations:

✔ respond to Yeats' assertion about what it means to be an artist?

✔ draw on specific text support?

Students are asked to explain how they feel about the opening line in Yeats' essay. It may help to begin by discussing what they feel sets painters, writers, musicians, or dancers apart from others.

READING AND WRITING EXTENSIONS

➤ Read students Franz Kafka's "A Hunger Artist" and have them compare his vision of the life of an artist with that of Yeats.

➤ Have students refer to the excerpts from James Joyce's *A Portrait of the Artist as a Young Man*, pages 93–99 and write about how Stephen's behavior as a child fits Yeats' description: "The poet's mind is in fact a receptacle for seizing and storing up numberless feelings, phrases, images."

Unit Overview

This unit focuses on five techniques of active reading: making predictions, drawing inferences, finding themes, rereading texts, and examining author's purpose. Practicing these strategies as they read and respond to writings by R. K. Narayan, Doris Lessing, and Frank O'Connor helps students to understand better what they read.

Literature Focus

	Lesson	Literature
1.	Thinking With the Writer	**R. K. Narayan,** "Trail of the Green Blazer" (Short Story)
2.	Reading Between the Lines	
3.	Thinking Theme	**Doris Lessing,** "Homage for Isaac Babel" (Short Story)
4.	Doubling Back	
5.	Author's Purpose	**Frank O'Connor,** from "Writing a Story—One Man's Way" (Nonfiction)

Reading Focus

1. The expectations that we bring to a story help us to make predictions before and during reading.
2. Making inferences about a story's characters will help you understand the characters' actions and motivations.
3. To find the theme of a piece, look at the subject of the story. Then try to analyze the author's attitude toward the subject.
4. Rereading and reflecting are essential to understand what an author means by a work and how the work relates to your own life.
5. Understanding the author's purpose will help you understand the author's message.

Writing Focus

1. Explain how making predictions helped you to become involved in a story.
2. Make inferences about characters based on details.
3. Summarize a story's theme.
4. Explain how you relate to a story's characters.
5. Rewrite a story as a four-line narrative.

One Thinking With the Writer

Critical Reading

FOCUS

Describing the art of a pickpocket, Raju explains, "The hunter in the forest could count his day a success if he laid his quarry flat; but here one had to extract the heart out of the quarry without injuring it."

BACKGROUND

Reading is not the passive activity that many students believe it to be. In fact, to get the most out of literature, readers need to question the text as they go along, pushing at it to make sense. For example, a reader begins the "Trail of the Green Blazer" with no idea of its setting. But reading details about people "in shirts and turbans, townsmen in coats and caps, beggars bare-bodied and women in multicouloured saris," an active reader puts the clues together and assumes the story is taking place in India. This may be an incorrect assumption, but it is a good, working premise. Plot details are similarly assembled. This story also engages readers by challenging the assumption that a pickpocket should be the bad guy in a story. In "Trail of the Green Blazer," the criminal is a much more sympathetic character than the victim.

FOR DISCUSSION AND REFLECTION

➤ Where did you first suspect that the day would not finish well for Raju? (Students should be able to notice early in the story that the man in the green blazer spells trouble for Raju.)

➤ Why do you think Raju refers to the man whose pocket he picks as the Green Blazer and "the other"? (Raju does this to keep himself from thinking about the victim as a person like himself. Raju is such a sensitive soul that as soon as he begins to think of this man as someone with a "motherless child," he does the unthinkable and tries to return the purse.)

➤ Though Narayan never describes Raju's home life, what do you think it must be like? What kind of a father do you think he is? (Many responses are possible, but students should point to Raju as a kind, loving, lively husband and father. Have students find the specific lines in the story that suggest these qualities of the man.)

Writing

QUICK ASSESS

Do students' responses:

✓ offer sensible predictions?

✓ explain how making predictions helped them to get involved in the story?

Students are asked to explain how making predictions helped them become involved in the world of Narayan's story. Help students to see that even incorrect predictions can help a reader become involved in the story.

READING AND WRITING EXTENSIONS

➤ Have students write a continuation for this story. What do they think Raju will do once he is released from prison?

➤ Invite students to write about an experience in which they—or someone they know—made a mistake and tried to correct it.

Two Reading Between the Lines

Critical Reading

FOCUS
Raju believed that "God had gifted the likes of him with only one-way deftness. Those fingers were not meant to put anything back."

BACKGROUND
R. K. Narayan was born in India and is widely regarded as the country's premier writer. Narayan has published many novels, including *Swami and Friends* and *The Guide*, as well as short story collections, including the celebrated *Under the Banyan Tree*. His work includes essays, travel books, and modern prose versions of the great Indian epics, the *Mahabharata* and the *Ramayana*.

FOR DISCUSSION AND REFLECTION
➤ What does Narayan's own attitude toward Raju seem to be? (In spite of Raju's faults and poor choice of profession, the writer seems to like the man very much. His tone conveys a fondness for the character.)

➤ Do you think Narayan is passing judgment upon either pickpocketing or the punishment of pickpockets in this story? (Many responses are possible, but students should see that the author is exploring the rich tapestry of human behavior and enjoying a chuckle at human foibles. The final lines of the story suggest that Raju has not been persuaded by his punishment to stop stealing but rather never again to put anything back.)

➤ How would this story be different if it were to be set in contemporary America? (Encourage students to explain how cultural differences would affect Narayan's plot and characters. For example, what does the fact that Raju is a professional pickpocket suggest about employment opportunities where he lives?)

Writing

QUICK ASSESS
Do students' charts:

✓ list actions or quotations that reveal the characters' personalities?

✓ draw inferences from these clues in the story?

Students are asked to chart actions or quotations for Raju and Green Blazer and then make inferences about what these lines demonstrate about the characters. Before they begin this exercise, have students make a list of actions or quotations for a well-known and well-liked person at your school or in your community. Then together draw inferences about this person from this evidence.

READING AND WRITING EXTENSIONS
➤ Have students read R. K. Narayan's story "House Opposite" and discuss how the hermit and the woman in the house represent opposing values in a way that is similar to the opposites of the Green Blazer and Raju in "Trail of the Green Blazer."

➤ Ask students to imagine that they are sharing a prison cell with Raju. Have them write an internal monologue for this character about his new cellmate, the pickpocket Raju.

Three Thinking Theme

C r i t i c a l   R e a d i n g

FOCUS

Isaac Babel said that "if I write seldom it is not because my life is hard but because it is uncertain, and this uncertainty derives entirely from changes and doubts connected with my work. I want to introduce into our literature new ideas, new feelings and rhythms. This is what interests me and nothing else."

BACKGROUND

Isaac Babel was a writer born in Odessa, Russia, in 1894. His work is unusual in that it is the fusion of four distinct traditions: Russian, Hebrew, Yiddish, and French. Besides the short stories for which he is most famous, Babel also wrote several plays and screenplays. Much of his work remains unpublished, untranslated, or lost. In fact, many of the details of Babel's life are uncertain and are mostly constructed from unsubstantiated theory and rumor. What is certain is that he was arrested in 1939 on unknown charges, a victim of Stalin's reign of terror, and is believed to have died in prison. In the story, "Homage for Isaac Babel," Doris Lessing uses a copy of Babel's short stories as a touchstone for her characters. Character is revealed through response to literature.

FOR DISCUSSION AND REFLECTION

➤ Why do you think Catherine picks up the copy of Isaac Babel stories in the first place? (Catherine is infatuated with Philip. She wants him to like her and thinks that reading what he is reading will help that to happen.)

➤ Based upon the narrator's description and Philip's behavior, what can you infer about his personality? (Philip is an intense, intelligent, somewhat arrogant young man. Like many fifteen-year-olds, he is quick to judge but also seems to care very much about injustice: "'But we've got to think about it, don't you see, because if we don't it'll just go on and *on*, don't you see?'")

➤ What do you think the narrator means when she says that she wishes "to protect this charming little person from Isaac Babel"? (Answers should include reference to the grim reality that Babel writes about that is utterly foreign to Catherine in her innocence. The narrator wishes she could put off the charming Catherine's awakening.)

W r i t i n g

QUICK ASSESS

Do students' responses:

✓ reflect a careful reading of the story?

✓ summarize the theme?

Students are asked to summarize the theme of this story. Have them work in pairs to craft a sentence that gets to the heart of what this story is saying about the power of literature to teach us about the world.

READING AND WRITING EXTENSIONS

➤ Ask students to imagine that they are a school friend of Catherine's. Have them write a phone conversation with Catherine following her visit to Philip's school, making reference to both the film and Isaac Babel's story.

➤ Have students research conditions in Stalinist Russia and contrast this political climate with Catherine's world.

Four Doubling Back

C r i t i c a l   R e a d i n g

FOCUS

Babel's knowledge of the powerful effect of conciseness in literature is revealed in a line from one of his stories: "There is no iron that can enter the human heart with such stupefying effect as a period placed at just the right moment."

BACKGROUND

In "Homage to Isaac Babel," Doris Lessing uses her own fiction to honor Babel's achievement in literature. Her narrator says of the writer, "He's a marvelous writer, brilliant, one of the very best." She also knows that Babel's stories may be difficult for a flighty teen to digest. When Catherine insists that "it's all morbid," the narrator tries to explain, "'But you have to understand the kind of life he had. First, he was a Jew in Russia. That was bad enough. Then his experience was all revolution and civil war and. . . .'" An unusual feature of "Homage to Isaac Babel" is the inclusion of the text of Catherine's thank-you letter. This document provides insight into Catherine and an ironic twist that Babel, who was famous for his sense of humor, would likely have enjoyed.

FOR DISCUSSION AND REFLECTION

➤ What did Catherine's and Philip's responses to the movie reveal to you about their characters? (Catherine responded emotionally and then wished to forget about what she had seen: "I think it's all absolutely beastly, and I can't bear to think about it." Philip, though dry-eyed, had a deeper response. As a reader of Isaac Babel's stories, he was able to comprehend the film's theme and message concerning capital punishment and man's inhumanity to man.)

➤ What does Catherine's letter to the narrator reveal about her character? (Students may mention her good manners, artificial diction, and preoccupation with Philip.)

➤ Why do you think teachers often assign depressing books like *The Grapes of Wrath, Beloved,* and Eli Weisel's *Night?* (Students should be able to see that for the truth to be told about certain eras, the stories will be depressing.)

W r i t i n g

QUICK ASSESS

Do students' responses:

✓ identify the character to whom they find it easiest to relate?

✓ explain the reason for their choice?

Students are asked to write about a character to whom they could relate. Before they begin, have the class brainstorm words and phrases about Catherine, Philip, and the narrator.

READING AND WRITING EXTENSIONS

➤ Ask students to choose a writer whose work has meant a great deal to them. Then ask students to write a story in which this author's novel, story, or poem appears. They should title the story "Homage to _____ ."

➤ Have students read "My First Goose" from Isaac Babel's *Collected Stories* and compare their reactions to the story to those of Catherine.

Five Author's Purpose

Critical Reading

BACKGROUND

In *The Art of Fiction: Notes on Craft for Young Writers,* John Gardner wrote that "What the beginning writer ordinarily wants is a set of rules on what to do and what not to do in writing fiction. Some general principles can be set down and some very general warnings can be offered, but on the whole the search for aethestic absolutes is a misapplication of the writer's energy. When one begins to be persuaded that certain things must never be done in fiction and certain other things must always be done, one has entered the first stage of aesthetic arthritis, the disease that ends up in pedantic rigidity and atrophy of intuition. Every true work of art—and thus every attempt at art—must be judged primarily, though not exclusively, by its own laws." In this excerpt from a lecture, Irish short story writer Frank O'Connor explains the rules he uses in his own composing process.

FOR DISCUSSION AND REFLECTION

➤ Based upon the tone and content of this excerpt, what kind of person do you think Frank O'Connor is likely to be? (Encourage students to speculate on whether he seems a talkative storyteller or a morose, tight-lipped brooder. Evidence in the excerpt seems to point to a natural storyteller with a gift for narrative.)

➤ Would you consider "Trail of the Green Blazer" to be a story that leaves you with a question or a story that answers a question that has been in your mind? (Have students explain why they feel as they do. If they don't believe the story does either, have them attempt to articulate how it is that "Trail of the Green Blazer" has affected them.)

➤ What purpose does seeing a story in four lines serve for O'Connor? (It allows him to examine the core of his story up close and to see if it is, in fact, something new or simply "a cutting from someone else's garden.")

Writing

Students are asked to rewrite either the Narayan or Lessing story as a four-line narrative. Have them talk with a partner about the essential elements of both plots before they begin to write.

READING AND WRITING EXTENSIONS

➤ Have students read Frank O'Connor's "The Duke's Children," the story to which he refers in his lecture.

➤ Ask students to describe their own process for writing an original story and then compare their descriptions with those of their classmates.

Unit Overview

The variety of techniques a storyteller uses to influence readers' responses is the subject of this unit. As students read and respond to the fiction of Sebastian Faulks, D. H. Lawrence, Iris Murdoch, and Anita Brookner, they will explore how writers dramatize tensions, encourage readers to empathize with characters, and experiment with different points of view and time frames.

Literature Focus

	Lesson	Literature
1.	Tension and Anticipation	**Sebastian Faulks,** from *Birdsong* (Novel)
2.	Empathy and Sympathy	
3.	Observer and Participant	**D. H. Lawrence,** from "England, My England" (Short Story)
		Iris Murdoch, from *The Unicorn* (Novel)
4.	Then and Now	**Anita Brookner,** from *Family and Friends* (Novel)
5.	Creating the Experience	

Reading Focus

1. A writer dramatizes the tensions of various actions and events so the reader will anticipate the outcome and experience the events along with the characters.
2. Readers respond emphathetically to various aspects of the story. The writer encourages them to experience the characters' situation.
3. Writers can make the reader a participant in or observer of the unfolding story.
4. Writers make use of various time frames as a story unfolds to control how the reader will experience and participate in the story.
5. Using different techniques to heighten anticipation and empathy will help a reader experience the events of a story.

Writing Focus

1. Describe an incident from your past, dramatizing the tension that surrounded it.
2. Continue a story by adding a scene to emphasize the character's feelings.
3. Explain how your stance as participant and observer affects your reaction to a story.
4. Shift the time frame and the point of view as you write about an event in a story.
5. Write about a personal experience using two of the techniques described in this unit.

One Tension and Anticipation

Critical Reading

FOCUS

Sebastian Faulks describing the tension of soldiers:

"The men on the floor of the tunnel stirred and dragged themselves back again into their crouching positions, in which they could again advance deeper."

BACKGROUND

Birdsong, by Sebastian Faulks, is the story of a soldier's struggle to survive the horrors of trench warfare in World War I and to find some meaning in the waste of millions of lives. The scenes that take place in the tunnels dug toward enemy lines by miners, who then set explosive charges, are among the most suspenseful in the novel. One of these has been excerpted here. Faulks' research into the technical reality is evident though not obtrusive. While others were being killed above ground, these soldiers had to deal with cave-ins, explosions, attacks of claustrophobia, and sheer exhaustion.

FOR DISCUSSION AND REFLECTION

➤ Which of your senses was the most stimulated by this excerpt? (Students should point to the lines in the text that affected them—for example, for the sense of smell: "Stephen could feel himself sweating. He could tell by the stench from the bodies packed in around him that he was not the only one.")

➤ How did Stephen's description of what he feared affect you as a reader? (Responses are likely to include students' identification with the feeling of being trapped and buried alive: "What had frightened him underground with Weir was when the earth fell behind them and he had for a moment thought he would not be able to turn round.")

➤ Can you think of other stories you have read in which the author creates this kind of tension? (One possible response, although different in so many ways from Faulks' writing, is the stories of Edgar Allan Poe.)

Writing

QUICK ASSESS

Do students' descriptions:

✔ focus on an experience of their own?

✔ effectively dramatize the tension of the incident?

Students are asked to write a description of an incident from their own experience, dramatizing the tension that surrounded the incident.

READING AND WRITING EXTENSIONS

➤ In the excerpt, Faulks writes that Evans worked "like an unwashed and unqualified doctor listening for signs of hostile life." Ask students to go back to what they have written about an incident from their own lives and insert a simile to describe what they were like in their stories.

➤ In order to compare what is happening above ground with what is happening below, have interested students research trench warfare in World War I and share their findings with the class.

Two Empathy and Sympathy

Critical Reading

FOCUS

Empathy is the ability to identify mentally with another person and, in so doing, to understand his or her feelings.

BACKGROUND

Sebastian Faulks' prose in *Birdsong* is both elegant and brutal. With the front virtually static for four years, and open combat between the sides suicidal because of all the firepower trained on the aptly named "no-man's land" between them, both sides began to form regiments of miners to tunnel toward each other. *Birdsong's* hero, Lieutenant Stephen Wraysford, served much of his long-term duty from the Somme to Armistice underground.

FOR DISCUSSION AND REFLECTION

➤ What does the moment when Stephen closes his eyes and wonders "whether, if he stayed in this position long enough, he might drift off to a final sleep" say to you about his state of mind? (Answers are likely to include discussion of how Stephen is tired of all the fighting and imagining what it might feel like to be dead.)

➤ Can you find evidence in the excerpt to indicate whether Stephen is new to war or somewhat experienced in its ways? (There are several references to how Stephen used to feel toward his men that suggest he has been fighting for some time, long enough to "remember this compassion, but he no longer felt it.")

➤ How do you think Stephen will react to Jack's discovery of footsteps in an enemy tunnel just above them? (Any well-supported answer is acceptable. Though Stephen has always done his duty before, he is showing signs of battle fatigue, including his daydream about the piece of timber just moments before Jack's announcement.)

Writing

QUICK ASSESS

Do students' scenes:

✓ continue from the last sentence of the selection?

✓ vividly portray characters' feelings and sensory details?

Students are asked to create the next scene in the tunnel, emphasizing the characters' feelings. Before they begin to write, talk about the possible scenarios that might emerge from the discovery that the enemy has a tunnel similar to their own just a few feet above their heads.

READING AND WRITING EXTENSIONS

➤ Read students Wilfred Owen's poem "Exposure" in which Owen and his freezing men are huddling in forward holes during a blizzard.

➤ At one point, Stephen guesses that his actions were meant to show his men "how fearless he was." Ask students to write a journal entry about a time in which they tried to act bravely in front of others.

Three Observer and Participant

Critical Reading

FOCUS
The narrator of a literary work is the person or voice that tells the story. The narrator can be a character in the story or a voice outside the action.

BACKGROUND
Most fiction employs third-person narrators, probably because they provide the most adaptable point of view. Third-person address assumes a neutral, or objective, presentation. The narrator is often presumed to be the author standing outside the events of the narration. This does not mean, however, that all third-person narrators are alike, for the author can choose the narrator's degree of involvement as well as the extent of his or her knowledge. He or she can be omniscient, with access to every thought and emotion of the characters, or can be only partially informed. An author can also restrict himself or herself to the position of pure observer, taking in and noting actions and conversations, but with no pretense of access to the characters' inner workings.

FOR DISCUSSION AND REFLECTION
➤ How would you describe the narrator in the excerpt from D. H. Lawrence's story, "England, My England"? (Students may mention the way this narrator remains outside the story, recording events for the reader to see and hear.)

➤ How did the third-person narration in the excerpt from Iris Murdoch's novel *The Unicorn* affect you? (Though outside the events being described, this narrator recounts an extremely charged moment in the story. Students will probably respond that the tension in this piece created more involvement for them than Lawrence's narrator achieved.)

➤ What kind of things can a third-person narrator do in a story that first-person and second-person narrators cannot? (Third-person narrators have more range and flexibility. They can go inside characters' minds and reveal events and information of which characters may be unaware.)

Writing

QUICK ASSESS
Do students' explanations:

✓ distinguish between the narrative stances in these two excerpts?

✓ comment on how this stance affects them as readers?

✓ include quotations from both passages?

Students are asked to compare the different effects achieved by D. H. Lawrence's and Iris Murdoch's narrative stances and to write about how they serve different purposes. Remind students that they must not only quote lines from the excerpts but also explain how these quotations support their theses.

READING AND WRITING EXTENSIONS
➤ Have students read Flannery O'Connor's short story "Everything That Rises Must Converge" and discuss the way in which, though the story employs a traditionally neutral third-person narrator, events are filtered through the protagonist's point of view.

➤ Ask students to imagine that they are Marian. Have them describe the experience recounted in the passage from *The Unicorn* from a first-person point of view.

Critical Reading

FOCUS

Anita Brookner's narrator judges Sofka harshly:

"I find it entirely appropriate and indeed characteristic that Sofka should have named her sons after kings and emperors and her daughters as if they were characters in a musical comedy."

BACKGROUND

In *Family and Friends*, Anita Brookner uses a first-person narrator who takes the reader along on her examination of a wedding photograph. A remarkable feature of this excerpt is the way the narrator seems to be speaking to readers as if they are sitting right by her side. It is as though the reader, too, is a character in the story along with the individuals described in the photograph. Brookner achieves this effect by having the narrator describe what she is seeing as she sees it: "Yes, Alfred must be the one on the right"; "And now I see that it is in fact a wedding photograph. The bride and groom were there all the time, in the centre, as they should be."

FOR DISCUSSION AND REFLECTION

➤ What do you think caused the narrator to miss the bride and groom at first glance? (Students may point to the narrator's fascination with Sofka and how this distracted her from what the photographer intended as the focal point of the picture.)

➤ What effect did the repetition of "I have no doubt" have upon you as you read? (It strongly suggests the narrator's stance toward what she observes in the photograph. This is a headstrong narrator, confident of her own interpretation.)

➤ Anita Brookner has had a dual career as an art historian and a novelist. How might her background of looking carefully at paintings and art have influenced how her narrator proceeds in this excerpt? (What the narrator seems to be doing in the story is scanning the wedding photograph, a technique for looking at works of art methodically and in great detail.)

Writing

QUICK ASSESS

Do students' writings:

✓ use the point of view of one of Sofka's children?

✓ use the present tense?

Students are asked to describe the wedding, in the present tense, from the point of view of one of Sofka's children. Encourage students to choose the character that most intrigued them and to use the act of writing from his or her point of view as a way to understand this character's feelings more deeply.

READING AND WRITING EXTENSIONS

➤ Have students find a wedding photo from a photo album or biography and write about the people in this picture the way Brookner has written about Sofka and her children.

➤ Read to students from the opening of Anita Brookner's Booker Prize-winning novel *Hotel du Lac* and compare the narrative stance with the excerpt from *Family and Friends*.

Five Creating the Experience

Critical Reading

FOCUS

FOCUS

William Stafford on the experience of reading:

"Readers should not be loaded with more information than a lively mind needs—puzzlement can be accepted, but insulting clarity is fatal."

BACKGROUND

In *You Must Revise Your Life*, William Stafford wrote, "Becoming a writer is just partly the learning of tricks and process of language. Literature comes about by way of a behavior, a way of thinking, a tendency of mind and feeling. We can all learn technique and then improvise pieces of writing again and again, but without a certain security of character we cannot sustain the vision, the trajectory of significant creation: we can learn and know and still not understand."

FOR DISCUSSION AND REFLECTION

➤ What did you learn from Sebastian Faulks' dramatization of tension in the excerpt from *Birdsong* that you could use in your own story? (Answers may include discussion of how, by recounting events in the tunnel from Stephen's point of view, Faulks puts readers in the same precarious circumstances that his character is in.)

➤ How did Faulks cause you to empathize with Stephen? (Rather than tell readers how his hero felt, Faulks describes Stephen's reactions to events in ways that cause readers to experience them along with him.)

➤ How did Brookner's use of multiple time frames involve you in her story? (Many responses are possible. Students may comment on how the reader is made to feel that he or she is making discoveries about the photograph right along with the narrator.)

Writing

QUICK ASSESS

Do students' stories:

✓ involve readers?

✓ use at least two of the techniques described in this unit?

Students are asked to write an episode from their own lives, using the techniques they learned from the first four lessons. It may help some writers to draw a storyboard of key events and then use this as a scaffold upon which to build their story.

READING AND WRITING EXTENSIONS

➤ Have students read Frank O'Connor's "My Oedipus Complex," a story told from the first-person point of view of a young boy who does not fully understand the events he describes. Ask students to speculate on how this differs from the first-person narrator in *Family and Friends*. (Brookner's narrator is confident that she understands much that the other characters do not.)

➤ Ask students to choose a photograph from the *Daybook* or from a magazine or newspaper. Have them use this picture as the inspiration for a brief story of their own. Suggest that they write about events that create tension and develop characters with which readers can empathize.

LANGUAGE AND STORY

Unit Overview

Both the literary selections and the writing assignments in this unit focus on "language play"—the attempt to have fun with and explore the limits of language. Students will study how Lewis Carroll, John Lennon, and Anthony Burgess use invented language and have an opportunity to experiment with language in their own writing.

Literature Focus

	Lesson	Literature
1.	Word Play	**Lewis Carroll,** "Jabberwocky" (Poetry)
2.	Language and Tone	**John Lennon,** "Randolf's Party" (Short Story)
3.	Reading Difficult Language	**Anthony Burgess,** from *A Clockwork Orange* (Novel)
4.	Language and Characterization	**Anthony Burgess,** from *A Clockwork Orange* (Novel)
5.	Creating Meaning Through Language	

Reading Focus

1. The reader can construct the sense of a story without knowing the specific meaning of each word.

2. Writers sometimes create words for fun and effect. The words often characterize the narrator and reveal his or her tone toward the subject.

3. Use various strategies—rereading, discussing, questioning, and sub-texting—as ways to make difficult language more accessible.

4. Writers use invented language to help reveal their characters' traits and qualities.

5. Experimenting with language for yourself is another way to understand the effects of language play on meaning.

Writing Focus

1. Describe a scenario that might have given rise to a poem.

2. Write a brief episode that relies heavily on made-up language.

3. Translate the invented language of a fictional passage.

4. Make assertions about characters based on the language they use.

5. Draft a story of your own that relies on language play to emphasize meaning.

One Word Play

Critical Reading

FOCUS

In the poem "Jabberwocky," Lewis Carroll explored ways to give sound a meaning as well as to give meaning to sound.

BACKGROUND

Sven Birkerts wrote that "Reading poetry can be an uncanny experience. The sounds and rhythms affect the reader in an almost bodily way; the contents, meanwhile, reach the mental and emotional self. At certain lucky moments, the poet is able to bring sound and meaning into a relation that sends a shiver up the reader's spine. This is what Emily Dickinson meant when she said a real poem made her feel as though the top of her head were coming off. This is the reason that a poem cannot be validly summarized—the meaning may be noted, but not the experience of the meaning." The connections between sound and meaning in poetry can be elusive, but it is important to remember that sound is one of the essential elements of poetry.

FOR DISCUSSION AND REFLECTION

➤ Some critics suggest that the sounds and rhythms of "Jabberwocky" remind readers of their own early efforts to master language. Do you agree? (Urge students who do agree to find lines from the poem that support their view.)

➤ To *jabber* means to talk rapidly and unintelligibly or to chatter like monkeys. How does Carroll's creative use of this word both in his title and in the name of his monster add to the poem's meaning? (These are two important clues to alert the reader that Carroll is playing with words and drawing associations that almost, but not quite, make sense.)

➤ What effect did the repetition of the first stanza as the last have on you as a reader? (Students may refer to the circular nature of children's tales as well as to Carroll's playful interest in sound and rhythm over sense.)

Writing

QUICK ASSESS

Do students' scenarios:

✔ explain who the poem is about and what happens?

✔ include some of the words from their charts?

Students are asked to write a description of who the poem is about and what situation might have inspired it. Remind students that there is no one correct interpretation of these images and that they should feel free to describe whatever pictures Carroll's words conjured up in their own minds.

READING AND WRITING EXTENSIONS

➤ Invite students to memorize a stanza from "Jabberwocky" and then hold a class performance of the poem.

➤ Have students read an excerpt from Gertrude Stein's "The Making of Americans" and compare her "nonsensical" language with that of Carroll.

Two Language and Tone

Critical Reading

FOCUS

Active readers can understand much about a narrator by paying attention to the language he or she uses.

BACKGROUND

When John Lennon was in school, he was a prankster who enjoyed getting in trouble. This may go some way to explaining why he took so many "grammatical liberties" in his writing. In 1964, Simon and Schuster published a collection of Lennon's writings titled *In His Own Write*, which included both prose and poetry reminiscent of "Jabberwocky."

FOR DISCUSSION AND REFLECTION

➤ Based on evidence from the text, what can you infer about Randolf's character? (Randolph lives alone, away from his family, and though he believes he has many "pals," is spending Christmas by himself.)

➤ How do his friends end up surprising Randolf? (Randolf welcomes them only to be murdered by the people he thought were his pals: "'We never liked you all the years we've known you. You were never raelly one of us you know, soft head.'")

➤ What message do you think John Lennon had in mind for readers when he wrote this story? (Responses will probably focus on the nature of false friends and the brutality that seems part of the society Randolf and his pals live in: "They killed him you know, at least he didn't *die* alone did he?")

Writing

QUICK ASSESS

Do students' episodes:

✓ include a variety of made-up language?

✓ convey the narrator's attitude through the language?

Students are asked to write a brief episode of their own that relies heavily on made-up language to characterize their narrator's attitude toward the subject. Help students get started by making a list of examples of onomatopoeia, words that sound like what they mean, on the board. Suggest that students adapt familiar onomatopoeic words— for example, "buzz," "tick-tock," "gong," and "click"—to their own purposes.

READING AND WRITING EXTENSIONS

➤ Have students read Robert Olen Butler's short story "Relic" from his Pulitzer Prize-winning collection *A Good Scent from a Strange Mountain*. It opens, "You may be surprised to learn that a man from Vietnam owns one of John Lennon's shoes."

➤ Ask students to work with a partner to compile a list of ten made-up compound words like Lennon's "aloneley." Suggest that they compose a short dialogue that uses as many of the words as possible.

Three Reading Difficult Language

Critical Reading

FOCUS

According to Burgess, "Nadsat, the Russified version of English that the characters speak, turns the book [*A Clockwork Orange*] into a linguistic adventure."

BACKGROUND

A Clockwork Orange is a brilliant and disturbing novel that creates an alarming vision of a future world full of violence, high technology, and authoritarianism. The central character, Alex, talks in a brutal invented slang designed to render his and his friends' social pathology. Anthony Burgess made up this teenage language he called Nadsat. It is English with a polyglot of slang terms and jargon thrown in. The main source for the additional terms is Russian although there are also contributions from French, Cockney English, Malay, Dutch, and Burgess' own imagination. Students may be interested to know that some editions of the novel include a glossary of terms.

FOR DISCUSSION AND REFLECTION

➤ How would you characterize Alex's relationship with his parents? (They seem to live in two different worlds. The parents know nothing of what Alex does at night and accept his evasive answers to questions about his "work." When Alex reminds his father that he never asks for money, "My dad was like humble mumble chumble.")

➤ Based on evidence from this excerpt, what kind of person does Alex seem to be? (Students should point to his confidence, cunning, and sense of self-reliance. He demonstrates a lack of respect for authority.)

➤ What kind of "work" do you speculate that Alex does when he leaves the house in the evenings? (Many responses are possible, but students may cite the fact that as Alex has been in a series of "Corrective Schools," it is likely that he gets into trouble most nights and that he is one of the "young hooligans" his father refers to who have taken over the streets.)

Writing

QUICK ASSESS

Do students' translations:

✔ reflect understanding of the plot?

✔ replace Alex's language with conventional English?

Students are asked to translate Alex's language into traditional English. Work out the first sentence together on the board.

READING AND WRITING EXTENSIONS

➤ Have students bring in samples of contemporary teenage slang—from magazines or song lyrics—and write about what these permutations of our language tell us of the attitudes of their creators.

➤ Invite students to view movies set in futuristic dystopias such as *Strange Days* or *Bladerunner* and compare these visions of the future with that of Burgess.

Four Language and Characterization

Critical Reading

FOCUS

William S. Burroughs on the writing of Anthony Burgess:

"I do not know of any other writer who had done as much with language as Mr. Burgess has done here."

BACKGROUND

Anthony Burgess wrote that "Clockwork oranges don't exist, except in the speech of old Londoners. The image was a bizarre one, always used for a bizarre thing. 'He's as queer as a clockwork orange' meant he was odd to the limit of oddness. I meant the title to stand for the application of a mechanistic morality to a living organism oozing with juice and sweetness." Recognized as one of the literary geniuses of our time, Anthony Burgess produced thirty-two novels, a volume of verse, sixteen works of nonfiction, and two plays. Originally a composer, his creative output also included countless musical compositions, including symphonies, operas, and jazz. Anthony Burgess died in 1993.

FOR DISCUSSION AND REFLECTION

➤ How would you describe Alex's relationship with his pals? (Alex has clearly been the leader up until now. In this passage, that role is being questioned by George. Alex is up to the challenge.)

➤ How does Alex's relationship with his chums differ from Randolf's in John Lennon's story? (Answers will vary, but Alex is clearly a more astute judge of human character. He senses danger in a heartbeat and rises to meet this danger with his own violence. Randolf seems to be a born victim.)

➤ What evidence does Alex use to support his position that he should be leader of the gang? (Alex contends that he is the one who comes up with the ideas for their escapades. He warns George and Will of the dangers of "'this sudden shilarny for being the big bloated capitalist.'" Alex is also ready to fight to reestablish his position.)

Writing

QUICK ASSESS

Do students' responses:

✓ make assertions about the characters based on their language?

✓ find evidence for these assertions within the text?

Students are asked to examine how language characterizes the narrator and his friends. Before they begin to look for supporting quotations, have students share their assertions about the characters. Encourage students to borrow from one another's ideas.

READING AND WRITING EXTENSIONS

➤ Have students read more from the novel *A Clockwork Orange*. The book jacket of some editions describes it as "a frightening fable about good and evil, and the meaning of human freedom. When the state undertakes to reform Alex to 'redeem' him, the novel asks, 'At what cost?'"

➤ Invite students to write the ending to this fight between Alex and George. Who do they predict will win? Why?

Five Creating Meaning Through Language

Critical Reading

FOCUS

From the beginning of Anthony Burgess' *A Clockwork Orange*:

"There was me, that is Alex, and my three droogs, that is Pete, Georgie, and Dim, Dim being really dim, and we sat in the Korova Milkbar making up our rassoodocks what to do with the evening."

BACKGROUND

Texts like "Jabberwocky" and *A Clockwork Orange* force a reader to work for meaning. When an interviewer once asked William Faulkner if he thought writers were under any obligation to their readers, Faulkner replied, "I don't care about John Doe's opinion on mine or anyone else's work. Mine is the standard which has to be met, which is when the work makes me feel the way I do when I read *La Tentation de Saint Antoine*, or the Old Testament. They make me feel good. So does watching a bird make me feel good."

FOR DISCUSSION AND REFLECTION

➤ Read the above quote from Faulkner to students and ask them to respond in terms of the texts they have read in the previous lessons. Did "Jabberwocky" make them feel good? Why or why not? (Accept all reasonable, supported responses.)

➤ What do you see as the possible dangers of making up words or combining familiar words in ways that will be unfamiliar to your readers? (Students may respond that readers may simply not be up to the challenge of figuring out what the writer is saying or that the writer could find it extremely difficult to use these made-up words consistently so that readers can decipher patterns of usage.)

➤ How did Alex's perspective shape your understanding of the excerpts from *A Clockwork Orange?* (As the narrator of the story, Alex is the only source of information for readers. The better that readers understand his character, the more accurately they can interpret the events he describes.)

Writing

QUICK ASSESS

Do students' stories:

✓ include a strong narrative voice?

✓ use language to emphasize the story's meaning?

✓ reflect creativity?

Students are asked to draft a story of their own that uses language play to emphasize its meaning. In order to help students determine their narrator's perspective, allow each to take turns in front of the class telling his or her story in the voice of the narrator. Encourage students to improvise on the spot.

READING AND WRITING EXTENSIONS

➤ Have students write an essay analyzing how Anthony Burgess used a made-up language to present readers with his vision of the future.

➤ Invite students to brainstorm a list of ten adjectives that describe one of their favorite places. Ask them to combine several of them in original ways to write a one-sentence description of the place they selected.

U n i t   O v e r v i e w

"Text and Context" is designed to help students discover the importance of knowing the contexts—historical, geographical, political, and personal—of the texts they read. Readings include poetry by Wilfred Owen, Richard Murphy, and Paul Durcan and nonfiction by Jamaica Kincaid.

L i t e r a t u r e   F o c u s

	Lesson	Literature
1.	Shifting Meanings With Allusions	**Wilfred Owen,** "Dulce et Decorum Est" (Poetry)
2.	The Context of Geography	**Richard Murphy,** "The Reading Lesson" (Poetry)
3.	Shifting Personal Perspectives	**Jamaica Kincaid,** "On Seeing England for the First Time" (Nonfiction)
4.	The Context of Politics	**Jamaica Kincaid,** "On Seeing England for the First Time" (Nonfiction)
5.	The Events of History	**Paul Durcan,** "Ireland 1972" (Poetry)

R e a d i n g   F o c u s

1. Active reading requires understanding how the context of an allusion can change the meaning.
2. The geography of a place can shape your view of events and characters in a literary work.
3. Memory of personal experiences can provide one perspective on events and ideas. Active readers must understand that the writer's perspective shifts when writing about memories.
4. Politics can play an important role in developing a writer's perspective. The reader's understanding of a writer's feelings comes from the text itself and from knowing the political context.
5. Multiple contexts can shape the writer's work. Considering several perspectives on the text can enrich your understanding of the author's message.

W r i t i n g   F o c u s

1. Imagine you are the speaker of a poem and write a letter describing your feelings.
2. Show how geographical details in a poem affect your perception of a character.
3. Write a story or poem describing a child's perspective of a place.
4. Analyze the final paragraph of an essay.
5. Write a poem using a specific historical event as context and subject.

One Shifting Meanings With Allusions

Critical Reading

FOCUS

In a letter home to his mother, Wilfred Owen described conditions at the front:

"The waders are of course indispensable. In two and a half miles of trench which I waded yesterday there was not one inch of dry ground."

BACKGROUND

Wilfred Owen's "Dulce et Decorum Est" protests the idea that dying for one's country is "sweet and honorable" by describing the agonizing death of one soldier caught in a gas attack during World War I. The speaker is a fellow-soldier, possibly someone much like Owen himself, who witnesses this death. The person the speaker ironically addresses as "My friend" is probably an older man who is busy patriotically recruiting teenage boys for the army. Owen's poem raises the question about whether it is always sweet and honorable to die for one's country.

FOR DISCUSSION AND REFLECTION

➤ Is the speaker in this poem an objective observer of the events being described or a subjective participant? (The pronoun *we* in line two alerts the reader that the speaker is himself a soldier and participant. The reference to his dreams suggests that some weeks or months have gone by since he witnessed the death that continues to haunt him. Draw students' attention to the fact that the first half of the poem is written in the past tense while the second half is written in the present tense. It is reasonable to speculate that the speaker has been furloughed back to England.)

➤ How do you interpret the simile in lines 13 and 14, "Dim, through the misty panes and thick green light, / As under a green sea, I saw him drowning"? (The phosgene gas used in World War I was greenish in color. The underwater effect is enhanced as the dying man is viewed by the other soldiers through the misty panes of their gas masks.)

➤ Do you believe there might be occasions where the saying *Dulce et decorum est pro patria mori* might hold true? (Encourage students to support their views with specific evidence.)

Writing

QUICK ASSESS

Do students' letters:

✓ reflect a careful reading of the poem?

✓ describe the poet's disillusionment?

Students are asked to write a letter from Owen to his family. Discuss the possibility that Owen might want to shield his family from some of the horrors he was experiencing.

READING AND WRITING EXTENSIONS

➤ Read to students from Paul Fussell's *The Great War and Modern Memory*, which describes the literary means by which World War I has been remembered and mythologized. Fussell explains in his preface that "I have focused on places and situations where literary tradition and real life notably transect, and in doing so I have tried to understand something of the simultaneous and reciprocal process by which life feeds materials to literature and returns the favor by conferring forms upon life."

➤ Have students write about occasions when they think it is sweet and honorable to die for one's country.

Two The Context of Geography

Critical Reading

FOCUS

The speaker in "The Reading Lesson" understands that "If books resembled roads, he'd quickly read: / But they're small farms to him, fenced by the page."

BACKGROUND

In "The Reading Lesson," Richard Murphy reflects upon how learning to read, something that most of us take for granted as a vital part of being alive, might be irrelevant to someone whose interests and sensibilities lie elsewhere. The poem is written from the point of view of a teacher attempting to instruct a fourteen-year-old boy on the rudiments of the alphabet. The boy seems impervious to the lessons, and the teacher wonders if he should give up. He realizes in the final stanza that if books had value to the boy, the youngster would snap them up in a moment. Rather than feeling as Emily Dickinson does that books are like frigates "to take us lands away," the boy feels "fenced by the page."

FOR DISCUSSION AND REFLECTION

➤ What do you think is the relationship between the speaker in the poem and the fourteen-year-old boy? (The speaker is someone attempting to teach the boy to read. In his failure, the teacher perceives that the boy has no use for reading—"'I'll be the same man whatever I do'"—and he begins to wonder if he shouldn't simply let the boy get on with his life. Literacy has no value or purpose in the boy's world.)

➤ Why do you think the speaker compares the boy's attitude toward reading with a mule's to a gap? (Students should note how the boy refuses to be led where others think he should go for his own good.)

➤ Based upon details in the poem, how would you characterize the kind of life that the boy leads? (Answers will vary, but students should make reference to the evidence that the boy is likely to become a thief, "Exploring pockets of the horny drunk / Loiterers at the fairs, giving them lice.")

Writing

QUICK ASSESS

Do students' paragraphs:

✓ explain how context influences their image of the boy?

✓ demonstrate a careful reading of the poem?

Students are asked first to rewrite the last stanza of the poem, changing the setting from Ireland to one with which they are familiar. Then they are asked to explain how the context of place affects the image of the boy. Before they write, have students sketch their image of the boy in the poem. How do they imagine he is dressed? What do they imagine he does the moment he leaves the schoolroom?

READING AND WRITING EXTENSIONS

➤ Have students imagine and then describe what their lives might be like had they never learned to read. How, like the boy, would there be "a field of tasks" they would "always be outside"?

➤ Ask students to research adult illiteracy. Have them think about why so many prison programs focus on teaching inmates to read.

Three Shifting Personal Perspectives

Critical Reading

FOCUS

Jamaica Kincaid explained that "I was always being told I should be something, and then my whole upbringing was something I was not: it was English."

BACKGROUND

Jamaica Kincaid grew up in the British colony of Antigua and was an eighteen-year-old when the country became self-governing. Antigua was finally granted its independence in 1981. Within the structure of the British educational system imposed upon Antiguans, Kincaid grew to "detest everything about England, except the literature." She felt first-hand the negative effects of British colonialism as the colonists attempted to turn Antigua into England and Antiguans into English without regard for the native culture. Though Kincaid has faced heavy criticism for her angry tone and simple writing style, she wears her anger like "a badge of courage," blaming her intimate connection to her homeland for creating "a sort of traumatic history."

FOR DISCUSSION AND REFLECTION

➤ What impact did the repetition of Kincaid's reference to seeing England for the first time in the opening sentence of each paragraph have on you as a reader? (Students may mention how Kincaid reminds readers at every step of her thesis. There is also something childlike about the repetition which Kincaid is consciously employing.)

➤ In what ways does Kincaid seem to blame her teacher for the image of England that Antiguans carry? (Kincaid describes the teacher's attitude toward England as reverential. The teacher said "'This is England'" with "authority, seriousness, and adoration, and we all sat up." The teacher imparts to the children her belief in England's superiority.)

➤ Where can you find evidence that Kincaid is critical of Antiguans? (Many responses are possible. Kincaid points to her father's felt hat and uses it as a metaphor for the many things Antiguans have adopted from the English that make no sense in this climate. Breakfast habits are another example.)

Writing

QUICK ASSESS

Do students' writings:

✓ depict the perspective of a young child who has never been to England?

✓ include details consistent with those which Kincaid presents?

Students are asked to write a story or poem entitled "I See England" from the perspective of an elementary school student who has never been to England. Before students begin to write, brainstorm the various sources of information about England that their narrator might be able to find.

READING AND WRITING EXTENSIONS

➤ Have students read Jamaica Kincaid's story "Girl," which is composed of a series of instructions from an Antiguan mother to her daughter on the threshold of growing up.

➤ Have students research another colonial writer who has had to come to terms with England's culture. Some possibilities include Derek Walcott, Edward Braithwaite, V. S. Naipaul, Patrick White, Salman Rushdie, Ben Okri, or Nadine Gordimer.

Four The Context of Politics

Critical Reading

FOCUS

Knowing the political context of a work provides readers with clues about its meaning.

BACKGROUND

In many ways, the identity Jamaica Kincaid has developed is a result of English upbringing and the lack of a native culture due to colonialism. She has said that nothing can erase her rage because "this wrong can never be made right." This undercurrent of rage at how colonialism warped Antiguan culture runs counter to the apparently charming simplicity of Kincaid's writing style. In fact, it is this contrast that makes her voice unique.

➤ Students may be interested to know Jamaica Kincaid was born Elaine Potter Richardson, but she changed her name because her family disapproved of her writing. Kincaid is a highly respected author who lives in Vermont where she now writes, gardens, teaches, and tends to her family, which includes two children.

FOR DISCUSSION AND REFLECTION

➤ Why does Kincaid say that the softer views of morning touching the sky and evening approaching were what made her "feel like nothing"? (These poetic images were so thoroughly at odds with the reality of Antigua's climate that reading them seemed to invalidate Kincaid's own perception of the world. Since whatever is English is always "right," the realities of Antigua must be "wrong.")

➤ What do you think is the significance of Kincaid's juxtaposition of the hymn "All Things Bright and Beautiful" with the portrait of the queen of England? (The hymn in praise of God's creations seems to be sung by permission from the monarchs.)

➤ How do you interpret Kincaid's statement that she was determined "to take from the world more than I give back to it"? (Many responses are possible, but students are likely to infer from this that Kincaid feels that she—and people like her—have given more than their share to the colonists' world and are now entitled to a better life.)

Writing

QUICK ASSESS

Do students' responses:

✓ demonstrate a careful reading of the poem?

✓ explain what happened when Kincaid's idea of England met the reality?

Students are asked to explain what happened in the final paragraph of Kincaid's essay, the moment when the idea of England met with the reality. If possible, play students the popular World War II song "The White Cliffs of Dover" or show them pictures of the landscape Kincaid describes.

READING AND WRITING EXTENSIONS

➤ Have students read one of Kincaid's essays on gardening from *The New Yorker*. Kincaid explains that, "Gardening is really an extended form of reading, of philosophy. The garden itself has become like writing a book. I walk around and walk around. Apparently people often see me standing there and they wave to me and I don't see them because I am reading the landscape."

➤ Ask students to write about a time when the image of something that they had carried for a long time in their minds contrasted with the reality.

Five The Events of History

Critical Reading

FOCUS

F.R. Higgins wrote that "Present-day Irish poets are believers—heretical believers, maybe—but they have the spiritual buoyancy of a belief in something. The sort of belief I see in Ireland is a belief emanating from life, from nature, from revealed religion, and from the nation."

BACKGROUND

Paul Durcan is one of Ireland's foremost contemporary writers. He has published sixteen collections of poetry and is the recipient of numerous literary awards, including the Patrick Kavanagh and Whitbread Poetry awards. He is probably best known outside literary circles for his contribution to the song "In the Days Before Rock & Roll" from Van Morrison's 1990 album *Enlightenment*.

FOR DISCUSSION AND REFLECTION

➤ Some critics believe that the function of poetry is not to tell us about experience but to allow us imaginatively to participate in it. How has Paul Durcan achieved this in his short poem "Ireland 1972"? (Though not informing the reader about the events he refers to, Durcan has succeeded in giving those readers who do have insight the feelings of those bloody days.)

➤ What did you infer from this poem about the two bodies? (Answers will vary, but students should point to the likelihood that the people died recently. While the "beloved grandmother" may or may not have died of natural causes, the speaker's "firstlove" who rests beside her was killed by his brother.)

➤ How is the poem a metaphor? ("Ireland 1972" is a metaphor for the human toll that political events have taken on the country. In addition, 1972 was one of the bloodiest years of the turmoil.)

Writing

QUICK ASSESS

Do students' poems:

✓ use Durcan's poem as a model?

✓ present a specific historical event as both context and subject?

Students are asked to write a poem using "Ireland 1972" as a model. Suggest to students that they are likely to need to generate many more than twenty words in order to find just the right ones to say exactly what they mean about a particular moment in time.

READING AND WRITING EXTENSIONS

➤ Ask students to research events in Ireland in 1972 and to report back to the class about how this information enriched their understanding of Paul Durcan's poem.

➤ Have students write about how having or lacking background information on World War I, English colonialism in the Caribbean, and Irish politics influenced their reading of the texts in this unit. Invite students to speculate on the connection between the study of history and the study of literature.

Unit Overview

In this unit, students will read and respond to the journalistic writing of Rebecca West and the nonfiction of C. S. Lewis. Students will develop their interpretive skills as they learn to recognize a writer's perspective, consider the writer's choice of words, and analyze the structure of an argumentative essay.

Literature Focus

	Lesson	Literature
1.	The Perspective of the Author	**Rebecca West,** from "Greenhouse with Cyclamens—I" (Nonfiction)
2.	Aspects of the Subject	
3.	Understanding an Opinion	**Rebecca West,** from "Greenhouse with Cyclamens—I" (Nonfiction)
4.	Reading an Argumentative Essay	**C. S. Lewis,** from *An Experiment in Criticism* (Nonfiction)
5.	Understanding Arguments	**C. S. Lewis,** from *An Experiment in Criticism* (Nonfiction)

Reading Focus

1. A writer's perspective often determines what facts are selected and how they are presented.
2. The choice of words and comparisons reveal the aspects of the subject that the author wants to emphasize.
3. Noticing the minor episodes and concrete images that writers use can help you interpret their broader meaning.
4. Understanding the structure of an argumentative essay helps you identify and respond to key points.
5. Trying to think like the author can help you understand his or her arguments.

Writing Focus

1. Explain your impressions of the objectivity of a piece of journalistic writing.
2. Describe a person you do not admire.
3. Explain how an episode or image reveals an author's views.
4. Write an argument of your own that defends or refutes an author's main point.
5. Write a description of yourself as a reader.

One The Perspective of the Author

Critical Reading

FOCUS

To many the Nuremberg War Crimes Trials indicated that transgressions against basic, universal human values would no longer be tolerated by the international community, and that a mechanism was now in place by which to hold people accountable for "crimes against humanity."

BACKGROUND

The Nuremberg War Crimes Trials stand as a landmark in international justice. To some they represent the application of fairness and equity; to others they reflect the imposition of a victor's justice on the vanquished. To all the bringing to public justice of Nazi leaders at the end of World War II marked a dramatic and unparalleled event in world history. Twelve prominent Nazis were sentenced to death. Rebecca West was sent to Nuremberg by *The New Yorker* to report on the proceedings for its readers.

FOR DISCUSSION AND REFLECTION

➤ Can you describe what is going on in the first long sentence of Rebecca West's essay? (West is on an airplane that is about to land in Germany, which had been associated for the past six years with death and destruction. Looking down, West is surprised to see such a benign visage on the "face of the world's enemy.")

➤ Why do you think West calls the courtroom a "citadel of boredom"? (A *citadel* is a fortress overlooking a city. West is describing how in the eleventh month of these trials everyone involved was past being shocked by evidence and was reasonably certain of the trials' outcome. As a result, the proceedings were in "the grip of extreme tedium.")

➤ Why do certain participants want the trials to go on forever while others want them to end as soon as possible? (Students should make clear that the defendants want the trial to go on forever to prolong their own lives while everyone else in the courtroom wants to be finished with this chapter of history and to get on with their own lives.)

Writing

QUICK ASSESS

Do students' responses:

✓ determine West's degree of objectivity?

✓ find evidence in the text that supports their view?

✓ explain how these examples demonstrate West's objectivity?

Students are asked to explain what it is in West's writing that determined for them her degree of objectivity. Some students may need to be reminded of the differences between an objective and a subjective point of view.

READING AND WRITING EXTENSIONS

➤ Ask students to imagine they are reporters at the Nuremberg War Crimes Trials. Write a letter home to a loved one about how observing the proceedings day after day is affecting them.

➤ Have students use books, encyclopedias, or the Internet to research the Nuremberg War Crimes Trials. Encourage students to think about whether the perspective of these authors is similar to that of Rebecca West.

Two Aspects of the Subject

Critical Reading

FOCUS
Analyzing an author's language provides clues about his or her meaning.

BACKGROUND
Rebecca West was the adopted name of Cicily Isabel Fairfied (1892–1983). She began calling herself Rebecca West at the age of nineteen, inspired by the feminist heroine in Henrik Ibsen's play *Rosmersholm*. West's first novel was *Return of the Soldier* (1918), which described the homecoming of a shell-shocked soldier after World War I. Her major nonfiction work, *Black Lamb and Grey Falcon* (1941), is a study of Yugoslavia; excerpts appeared in *The Atlantic Monthly*. Students may be interested to know that current political unrest in the Balkans has renewed interest in the work.

FOR DISCUSSION AND REFLECTION
➤ How would you characterize West's portrayals of the Nazi defendants? (Some students may find her descriptions brutally harsh while others may feel she demonstrates too much sympathy. Whatever their opinions, have students support them with evidence.)

➤ Why do you think West chose to describe Goering, Hess, and Schacht as she did? (Students' answers to this will be related to their response to the previous question. Help students to see how West emphasizes their human traits rather than their deeds. Hess is clinically insane. Schacht is arrogant and "petrified by rage." Goering is soft and "infinitely corrupt.")

➤ The Nuremberg Trials were construed by many at the time as an auspicious sign of world healing after World War II. In your opinion, what purpose did such a public display serve? How might testifying as to their guilt assuage the suffering of some of the victims of Nazi terror? (Many responses are possible. Students may not be familiar with the extent to which Nazi war crimes were detailed through the course of the trial.)

Writing

QUICK ASSESS
Do students' webs:
✔ focus on one trait of a character they do not admire?
✔ contain words and phrases that describe the person?

Students are asked to compose a composite word picture of a person they do not admire. This character may be someone they know personally or someone they have only heard or read about.

READING AND WRITING EXTENSIONS
➤ Show students the movie *Judgment at Nuremberg* and compare the filmmakers' interpretation of events with that of Rebecca West.

➤ Have students recall a sporting event they witnessed in which they had a very strong opinion about who they wanted to win. They should attempt to write an objective account of this game and then read what they have written to a partner to see if their bias is obvious.

Three Understanding an Opinion

Critical Reading

FOCUS

From "Greenhouse with Cyclamens—I":

"If a trial for murder lasts too long, more than the murder will out. The man in the murderer will out; it becomes horrible to think of destroying him."

BACKGROUND

In his biography of Rebecca West, Carl Rollyson has written that West's "approach to reality was biographical in the sense that she gave it a personality that could be analyzed. The biographical mode endowed her with enormous explanatory power over events that others might consider too complex, too confused, too chaotic to reduce to the form of a plot, a conspiracy, or a psychological theory. She could be wildly wrong about a person, a people, an incident; she could also be extraordinarily prescient."

FOR DISCUSSION AND REFLECTION

➤ Do you agree or disagree with Rebecca West when she says that "when society has to hurt a man it must hurt him as little as possible and must preserve what it can of his pride, lest there should spread in that society those feelings which make men do the things for which they get hanged"? (Answers will vary depending upon students' views of crime and punishment but should demonstrate an understanding of West's point that society must hold itself to the highest standards of behavior.)

➤ Why do you think the judge's wife, after attending most of the previous sessions, chose not to be there for the verdicts? (Students should point to her reluctance to witness the moment when society passes judgment.)

➤ What is the significance of the two Greek statues for Rebecca West? (For West, these are examples of "the whole truth about certain moments of physical existence" that have survived all the horror that has gone on around them in Germany. They are models of what society must strive to preserve. West points to the statues as reminders of what is best in human beings.)

Writing

QUICK ASSESS

Do students' responses:

✓ focus on one episode or image?

✓ comment on West's thoughts about human nature and capital punishment?

Students are asked to explain how one specific episode or image relates to Rebecca West's thoughts about human nature and capital punishment.

READING AND WRITING EXTENSIONS

➤ Have students read Bernhard Schlink's *The Reader*, a contemporary novel about the trial of a female Nazi war criminal many years after the war.

➤ West describes the sadness of a judge's wife as the trials came to an end by saying that "she was living through a desert of time comparable to the interval between a death and a funeral." Ask students to compose other similes to describe such a time of sorrow.

Four Reading an Argumentative Essay

Critical Reading

FOCUS

From *The Rhetoric of Fiction* by Wayne Booth:

An ideal reader "should use his mind, his critical intelligence, as well as his emotions."

BACKGROUND
Clive Staples Lewis (1898–1963) was a literary scholar, critic, and novelist. Students may be familiar with his fantasy stories about the world of Narnia, including *The Lion, the Witch, and the Wardrobe*. In this excerpt from *An Experiment in Criticism*, Lewis suggests that rather than holding books up to be measured, we should hold up readers for sizing. Instead of looking for what is right or wrong in books, Lewis looks at what is right and wrong in readers.

FOR DISCUSSION AND REFLECTION
➤ Why do you think some critics of Lewis have called him an elitist? (Students should identify in the essay repeated references to the "majority" and the "minority." At every step, Lewis includes himself and the reader of the essay as members of this second group of good readers.)

➤ What are some of the habits that Lewis ascribes to the "majority" of readers? (They never read anything twice. They "do not set much store by reading" and turn to it as a "last resource." They have never been shaken to the core by a piece of literature. They seldom think or talk about what they are reading.)

➤ How do the habits of readers such as Lewis differ from those of the "majority"? (Student responses are likely to be shaped by their own reading habits. Lewis claims that readers like himself often reread great works, are always on the lookout for time to read, feel bad when they go too long without reading, and use what they have read to help them reflect upon their own lives.)

Writing

QUICK ASSESS

Do students' arguments:

✓ formulate an opinion regarding Lewis' thesis?

✓ explain their opinion using evidence from their own experience?

Students are asked to write an essay that either defends or refutes Lewis' premise regarding readers. Check that every student has fully understood his points before they begin to argue for or against them.

READING AND WRITING EXTENSIONS
➤ Have students read and respond to one of two poems about reading—Philip Larkin's "A Study of Reading Habits" or Wallace Stevens' "The House was Quiet and the World was Calm."

➤ Ask students to describe the ideal conditions for them to read including time of day, place, position, atmosphere, and state of mind.

Five Understanding Arguments

Critical Reading

FOCUS

Henry James explained that what the author does is to "make his reader very much as he makes his characters. When he makes him ill, that is, makes him indifferent, he does no work; the writer does ill. When he makes him well, that is, makes him interested, then the reader does quite half the labor."

BACKGROUND
Wayne Booth explains that "if we want to deal with an ideal literature that has never existed on land or sea, and postulate an ideal reader who could never possibly exist, and then judge all books and all readers as they more or less approximate this pure state, that is our privilege. But as the facts are, even the greatest of literature is radically dependent on the concurrence of beliefs of authors and readers."

FOR DISCUSSION AND REFLECTION
➤ Do you agree with Lewis that "readers are already foreshadowed in the nursery"? (Many responses are possible. Encourage students to share stories about people who have either always loved to read or who only came to books later in life.)

➤ How do you think that classroom teachers can encourage students to read difficult books? (Students' answers will depend on their experiences. Encourage students to separate idiosyncratic bad experiences from generalizations about learning how to read challenging texts.)

➤ Where do you think Lewis would stand on the subject of assigned summer reading? (Encourage students to discuss whether summer should be a time for students to choose their books freely. There are arguments to be made on either side.)

Writing

QUICK ASSESS

Do students' writings:

✓ offer a general description of themselves as readers?

✓ identify particular characteristics?

Students are asked to describe themselves as readers. Before they begin to write, have students recall stories about themselves and books—for example, how they learned to read or how they used to demand one particular book before bedtime every night. Suggest that such stories belong in any analysis of their own reading habits.

READING AND WRITING EXTENSIONS
➤ Read to students from Lynne Sharon Schwartz's book *Ruined by Reading*, in which this novelist explores the ways in which reading has shaped her life. Help students to see that her book-length argument clearly supports Lewis' premise though she accomplishes this without being quite so critical of recreational reading as the Oxford don seems to be.

➤ Have students write about a book whose reading came closest to achieving what Lewis described as "an experience so momentous that only experiences of love, religion, or bereavement can furnish a standard of comparison."

CHARACTER IN POETRY

Unit Overview

"Character in Poetry" presents students with three poetic portraits to study and enjoy—a sonnet by George Barker, a dramatic monologue by Robert Browning, and one by W. H. Auden. Students will explore how poets use figurative language and second person and how they vary the tone and style to develop rich characters.

Literature Focus

	Lesson	Literature
1.	Understanding Character	**George Barker,** "To My Mother" (Poetry)
2.	The Dramatic Monologue	**Robert Browning,** "My Last Duchess" (Poetry)
3.	Reading a Long Poem	**W. H. Auden,** "In Memory of W. B. Yeats" (Poetry)
4.	Direct Address	**W. H. Auden,** "In Memory of W. B. Yeats" (Poetry)
5.	Completing the Reading	**W. H. Auden,** "In Memory of W. B. Yeats" (Poetry)

Reading Focus

1. Writers use metaphors and allusions as a way to create a well-defined portrait.
2. A dramatic monologue is structured to focus your attention on the character of the speaker as he or she unintentionally reveals it in the course of the poem.
3. Asking yourself questions and attempting to answer them is a useful strategy in dealing with complex pieces of literature. Work through the possible answers to your questions until you feel confident in your understanding.
4. The use of the second person draws us into the poem and makes us read both as ourselves and as the subject being addressed in the poem.
5. The long poem generally focuses on a subject from a variety of angles, leading the reader toward an idea or theme through all the sections of the poem.

Writing Focus

1. Write four or five similes to describe the mother.
2. Write a character sketch of the speaker of "My Last Duchess."
3. Describe the signifance of the various landscapes depicted in the beginning of Auden's poem.
4. Reflect on the meaning of a line in a poem.
5. Comment on Auden's views on Yeats, poetry, and art in general.

One Understanding Character

Critical Reading

FOCUS

Creating metaphors for a character in a poem, story, or novel is a useful strategy as it lets you visualize what this person is like from a number of different perspectives.

BACKGROUND

Character in poetry is often revealed obliquely. The reader must infer from allusions, metaphors, and images what the person was like. Just studying the nature of a poem's narrator is a study in character as the poet reveals a great deal of information about a narrator by controlling tone, stance, diction, and the selectivity of detail. While in some poems, the development of a character may seem almost incidental to the ideas the poet is presenting, in others the character emerges as richly drawn and memorable.

FOR DISCUSSION AND REFLECTION

➤ How do the similes and metaphors build the character of the woman in the poem? (Responses might include, for example, that the phrase "Irresistible as Rabelais" means that the narrator sees his mother as "bigger than life" but very down-to-earth at the same time. Explain to students that Rabelais was a sixteenth-century scholar, physician, and writer who wrote extravagantly and honestly about the lives and loves of everyday people.)

➤ How did you interpret the lines "She is a procession no one can follow after / But be like a little dog following a brass band"? (His mother's presence is so imposing that to walk behind her is to walk in her wake and let her power carry you along.)

➤ What do the references to "the bomber" and "a cellar" tell you about the setting of this poem? (During World War II, Germans bombed the British Isles night after night. The speaker describes how his mother refused to go to the bomb shelter to safety with the others and instead leaned "on the mahogany table like a mountain / Whom only faith can move . . . .")

Writing

QUICK ASSESS

Do students' comparisons:

✓ reflect understanding of the mother?

✓ include four or five metaphors or similes?

Students are asked to create additional similes and metaphors for the character in George Barker's poem "To My Mother." After students have worked for a few moments, have them share what they have come up with. Look especially at the metaphors they create using animals, plants, seasons, colors. A discussion of their reasoning for their choices will take them back to the poem with greater insight.

READING AND WRITING EXTENSIONS

➤ Ask students to write a poem modeled after "To My Mother" in which they explicitly use similes and metaphors as Barker does as he creates the picture of his mother. They should choose a person who is important to them and dedicate the poem to that person.

➤ Have students reread "I Think Continually of Those" by Stephen Spender (page 79) and discuss the writer's use of metaphor in the poem.

Two The Dramatic Monologue

Critical Reading

FOCUS

Robert Browning's poem "My Last Duchess" is a masterpiece of dramatic irony wherein the reader knows more about the duke than he knows about himself.

BACKGROUND

In "My Last Duchess," a dramatic monologue by Robert Browning, the speaker is the Duke of Ferrara. The time is the late Italian Renaissance, probably mid-sixteenth century. The place is an upper room in the duke's palace. The audience is an envoy from a count whose daughter the duke plans to marry. The occasion is that the duke and the count's emissary have just concluded negotiations over the terms of the marriage and the dowry that the duke expects to receive with his bride. On the way to join the company of guests in the hall below, they pass a portrait of the duke's former wife, and the duke pauses to display it for the emissary.

FOR DISCUSSION AND REFLECTION

➤ Based upon his monologue, how would you characterize the duke? (Many responses are possible, but students should focus on the man's pride and his cruelty. His dissatisfaction with his former wife was that instead of being lofty like him, thus enhancing the eminence of his station, she treated inferiors as equals and was pleased when they did her favors. Were it not for the "stooping," the duke would not hesitate to tell his wife that this "in you disgusts me." It is implied that he had her put to death.)

➤ What do the references to art tell the reader about the duke? (He is a connoisseur of art, yet his love of painting and painters reflects his pride. Part of the value of his Neptune taming a sea-horse is that it is "thought a rarity.")

➤ How does Browning make use of dramatic irony in this poem? (The duke speaks all the words, seeking to offer a favorable impression of himself, yet the reader comes away with a fondness for his last duchess and a feeling of total repugnance for the duke.)

Writing

QUICK ASSESS

Do students' character sketches:

✓ demonstrate understanding of the duke's personality and motives?

✓ draw on specifics from the text?

Students are asked to write a character sketch of the duke. In order to help the duke come to life, it may help to have students improvise a scene between him and his last duchess while they were still married.

READING AND WRITING EXTENSIONS

➤ Invite students to imagine a contemporary husband walking a friend past a photograph of his last wife. Have them write a dramatic monologue for this husband based upon the premise that he is quite glad she is gone.

➤ Have students find other dramatic monologues and note the characteristics of the genre.

Three Reading a Long Poem

Critical Reading

For background information on W. B. Yeats, see "Focus on the Writer: William Butler Yeats," pages 101–12.

FOCUS

An elegy is a song or poem expressing sorrow and lamentation for one who has died.

BACKGROUND

W. H. Auden grew up in a scientific rather than literary atmosphere. His education followed the standard pattern for children of the middle and upper-middle classes in England, and in 1925 he entered Oxford University. There Auden exerted a strong influence on other literary intellectuals such as C. Day-Lewis, Louis MacNeice, and Stephen Spender. Spender printed by hand the first collection of Auden's poems in 1928. Upon graduating from Oxford in 1928, Auden lived for a year in Berlin, then spent the next five years working as a schoolmaster in Scotland and England.

➤ For background information on W. B. Yeats, see "Focus on the Writer: William Butler Yeats," pages 101–12.

FOR DISCUSSION AND REFLECTION

➤ In what way do you perceive that William Butler Yeats is "scattered among a hundred cities"? (Many responses are possible, but students are likely to point to the way Yeats' poems have spread around the world. The "words of a dead man" have a life of their own.)

➤ What do you think Auden is saying in the fifth stanza about the future of Yeats' poems and reputation? (He believes that even in the "importance and noise of to-morrow," a few thousand readers will still look back on this day when Yeats died and mourn the loss of a great poet.)

➤ What effect did the repetition of lines 5 and 6 as the final lines of this section have on you as a reader? (The repetition brings the reader back full circle to Auden's thesis. Both this refrain and the opening "O" give the elegy a song-like quality.)

Writing

QUICK ASSESS

Do students' responses:

✓ list a variety of landscapes described in the first part of the poem?

✓ describe how the landscapes relate to the death of Yeats?

Students are asked to make a list of the various landscapes depicted in the first part of "In Memory of W. B. Yeats" and then to relate these images to the poet's death. Tell students not to worry if their explanations seem far-fetched. What is important here is for them to learn how to speculate about possible connections between imagery and meaning.

READING AND WRITING EXTENSIONS

➤ Have students choose a famous person whose death they can remember and write about the day this person died, using various landscape images as Auden has done.

➤ Ask students to turn back to pages 101-12 to reread William Butler Yeats' poetry.

Four Direct Address

Critical Reading

FOCUS

W.H. Auden describing his elegies on Freud and Yeats:

"These elegies of mine are not poems of grief. Freud I never met, and Yeats I only met casually and didn't particularly like him. Sometimes a man stands for certain things, which is quite different from what one feels in personal grief."

BACKGROUND

In 1939, at age thirty-one, W. H. Auden arrived in New York City. Two days later, on January 28, Yeats died in southern France. Shortly after, Auden wrote "In Memory of W. B. Yeats" and a prose piece called "The Public vs. the Late Mr. William Butler Yeats." In this essay, Auden debates whether or not Yeats deserved to be considered a great poet. In the poem, which was published on March 8, 1939, in the *New Republic*, Auden does not weep nor does he tempt the reader to do so. The poem has no pleasing description of Yeats nor a sense of personal debt. Auden does, however, note that Yeats' "gift survived." By modifying the expected praise and passion with ambivalence and emotional reserve, Auden has written a modern version of the elegy.

FOR DISCUSSION AND REFLECTION

➤ How did you interpret the line "mad Ireland hurt you into poetry"? (Answers are likely to include discussion of how the culture shaped Yeats as a man and as a result, influenced his poetry. The images of Ireland are negative and menacing.)

➤ Why do you think Auden might choose to address this movement of his elegy directly to Yeats? (Many responses are possible, but they should focus on Auden's identification with Yeats as a poet—"You were silly like us." It can be argued that Auden uses this elegy to Yeats to reflect upon his own poetry.)

➤ Do you believe that "poetry makes nothing happen"? Do you think Auden believes it or wants his readers to? (Students' answers probably will vary widely. Ask students to think about why, if "poetry makes nothing happen," does it continue to be written and read? Auden admits that "it survives.")

Writing

QUICK ASSESS

Do students' responses:

✔ explain what Auden meant by "poetry makes nothing happen"?

✔ reflect what Auden is saying about Yeats?

Students are asked to explain what they think Auden's phrase "poetry makes nothing happen" means within the context of the poem. It is important to have students compare this phrase with the final lines of this section of the poem, in which Auden states that poetry "survives, / A way of happening, a mouth."

READING AND WRITING EXTENSIONS

➤ Have students read Percy Bysshe Shelley's "Adonais," an elegy for John Keats. Ask students to compare this traditional approach to the form with that of Auden.

➤ In this section of "In Memory of W. B. Yeats," Auden points to Ireland as having shaped both Yeats and his poetry. Ask students to write about how the politics and geography of where they live might shape their work were they to become poets.

Five Completing the Reading

C r i t i c a l   R e a d i n g

FOCUS

John Fuller has written that "The real point about the value of art that Auden is making is that it teaches 'the free man how to praise.'"

BACKGROUND

In the poem "In Memory of W. B. Yeats," Auden has modernized the pastoral elegy of Milton and Shelley by adding urban images and narrative voices and modified the expected praise with ambivalence and emotional reserve. Auden's poem also substitutes the idea of a soul's eternal life with comments about a poem's purpose and lasting effect. The first movement is in free verse. There is no fixed line length and no end rhyme. The second movement is full of slant rhyme: "all-still," "decay-poetry," "survives-executives." The final movement contains exact rhymes like "dark-bark" and "wait-hate." Students may notice that the rhythm in this section is that of hymns and children's songs.

FOR DISCUSSION AND REFLECTION

➤ How did the shift in rhythm affect you as a reader? (Students are likely to mention the way the powerful rhythm is reminiscent of what occurs in a song. To some, this may suggest a funeral march or church hymn. Compared with the earlier passages, this section is both ponderous and precise.)

➤ Why do you think Auden gives instructions to the earth? (He tells the earth to "receive an honoured guest," one who has earned his rest through service in poetry.)

➤ What did you infer from Auden's instructions to Yeats to "Follow, poet, follow right / To the bottom of the night . . ."? (Many answers are possible. Auden seems to be enjoining Yeats to continue to "persuade us to rejoice" even from the dead. Though the poet is gone, the poem "survives.")

W r i t i n g

QUICK ASSESS

Do students' writings:

✓ explain what Auden is saying about Yeats?

✓ comment on what the poem suggests about poetry and art in general?

Students are asked to explain what Auden is saying about Yeats, about poetry, and about art in general. Draw their attention to the phrase in the third section in which Auden writes of "the farming of a verse." One place for students to begin might be to compare a poet working with language to a farmer working the land.

READING AND WRITING EXTENSIONS

➤ Have students read "Lullaby," another W. H. Auden poem with strong rhythm and rhyme.

➤ Ask students to write an elegy to an author or poet who has influenced how they think about the world.

Unit Overview

In "Poetry and Art," students are invited to explore poems by Percy Bysshe Shelley, John Keats, Kaoru Maruyama, and T. S. Eliot. As they improve their abilities to understand irony, visualize scenes, recognize ambiguity, and compare poems, students will deepen and expand their understanding and appreciation of the poetry they read.

Literature Focus

	Lesson	Literature
1.	The Art of Irony	**Percy Bysshe Shelley,** "Ozymandias" (Poetry)
2.	Visualizing a Poem	**John Keats,** "Ode on a Grecian Urn" (Poetry)
3.	Discovering Possible Interpretations	**John Keats,** "Ode on a Grecian Urn" (Poetry)
4.	Comparing Poems	**Kaoru Maruyama,** "A Rhinoceros and a Lion" (Poetry)
5.	Exploration and Interpretation	**T. S. Eliot,** from "Burnt Norton" from *Four Quartets* (Poetry)

Reading Focus

1. Writers use irony to point out the differences between what is imagined and what is.
2. Visualizing a scene depicted by a writer is an important step toward understanding the meaning.
3. Poetry is often ambiguous. It is important to keep all the possibilities of interpretation open as you read and think about a poem.
4. Comparing poems on the same theme is a way of gaining new perspectives on them.
5. An interpretation of a poem needs to be based on both analysis and reflection. Exploring the language and ideas of a poem will help you solidify your ideas and construct your interpretation.

Writing Focus

1. Explain a poet's use of situational irony.
2. Create a scene that expresses Keats' idea that in art all things are possible.
3. Interpret a poem, being sure to include quotations to support your ideas.
4. Compare and contrast two poems with a similar theme.
5. Create a "found poem" using words and phrases from "Burnt Norton" and then comment on what you have learned about Eliot's poem.

One The Art of Irony

Critical Reading

FOCUS

In "Ozymandias," the insight of the artist has outlasted the power of the conqueror.

BACKGROUND

The central theme of Percy Bysshe Shelley's "Ozymandias" is the vanity of tyrants who assume their glory will last forever. This theme is brilliantly conveyed through irony of situation: expectation is turned on its head by events. Increasing the irony is that the sole remaining work of this self-proclaimed "king of kings" is a huge broken statue, carved by an artist who saw through the self-deluding egocentrism of the ruler and recorded it in stone, mocking Ozymandias, as it were, to his face. No English person in 1817 could have read this poem without thinking of Napoleon, who had conquered almost all of Europe before he was defeated at Waterloo in 1815. Contemporary readers may be reminded of Hitler, Mussolini, Stalin, or Mao.

FOR DISCUSSION AND REFLECTION

➤ How would you put the inscription on the pedestal into your own words? (One possible approximation would be "Look at the things I have accomplished, you mighty though lesser kings, and forget about ever matching them.")

➤ What is the situational irony inherent in this inscription? (One would expect to look up from reading such a statement and see a great imperial city with monuments, palaces, and temples. Instead, as far as the eye can see, there is only emptiness and sand.)

➤ Did Ozymandias remind you of any contemporary people? (Many responses are possible. Students are likely to think of figures from big business, rock music, and the sports world as examples of individuals who think their power and influence will last forever.)

Writing

QUICK ASSESS

Do students' responses:

✔ explain Shelley's commentary on power, time, and art?

✔ reflect how Shelley has used situational irony to make his point?

Students are asked to write about how Shelley has used irony to comment on power, time, and art. Before students begin, make a chart on the board of lines and phrases from the poem that refer to each of these three issues. Some lines may appear in more than one column.

READING AND WRITING EXTENSIONS

➤ Have students research Napoleon's conquest of Europe (or another dictator's exploits) and report back to the class on how his attitude resembled that of Ozymandias.

➤ Ask students to construct a contemporary parallel to the story the traveler tells. Have students write what he or she might report back after making observations.

Two Visualizing a Poem

Critical Reading

FOCUS
Like other poems by John Keats, "Ode on a Grecian Urn" explores the human desire to escape the inevitable effects of living in a temporal world.

BACKGROUND
"Ode on a Grecian Urn" is a meditation on the continuing beauty of a painted vase from classical Greece and what it seems to communicate to a man who knows that, by comparison, his time on earth is brief. The structure of the poem is a dramatic enactment of the stages of the speaker's emotional and imaginative progress. The ode opens with the speaker praising the urn's calm stillness and its freedom from the ravages of time. In the second stanza, possibly as a result of not having his questions answered, the speaker's attitude seems to shift. He now prefers not to hear the narrative facts that the urn refuses to reveal anyway and instead relishes the "unheard melodies" of feelings without explicit meanings. The third stanza extends the speaker's delight in the image of time stopped at the height of anticipated bliss.

FOR DISCUSSION AND REFLECTION
➤ What denotations and connotations can you apply to Keats' use of "still" in the first line? (Students should point to Keat's pun. The urn is both silent and unmoving, and it "still" exists in time.)

➤ How do you interpret the pastoral scene described in lines 15–20? (Encourage students to visualize and sketch what Keats describes before they attempt to interpret the speaker's meaning. The speaker celebrates the fact that this amorous pursuit will never end. Since the lovers are permanently frozen in a painting, the youth will continue to exist in his state of anticipation just as her beauty will never fade.)

➤ How is the reference to "happy boughs! that cannot shed / Your leaves" important to Keats' theme? (The trees depicted on the urn will be forever green and live in an unending spring. Urge students to discuss the implications of such a condition.)

Writing

QUICK ASSESS
Do students' scenes:

✓ express Keats' idea that in art all things are forever possible?

✓ reflect careful thought and creativity?

Students are asked to create a scene reflecting on Keats' idea that in art, all things are forever possible. Because students' experiences with art will vary so widely, it may help them to browse through art books from the school library before they begin to write. Encourage students to let one of the paintings or statues that they see be the focus for their scenes.

READING AND WRITING EXTENSIONS
➤ Ask students to bring in reproductions of pieces of art that have affected them deeply and then have them write about the musings that these works have inspired. Ask students to show and tell others in the class about their painting or sculpture.

➤ Read to students from Robert Hughes' collection of essays about art, *Nothing If Not Critical*. Discuss together how this critic's attitude toward art is similar to and different from Keats' attitude.

Three Discovering Possible Interpretations

Critical Reading

FOCUS

From a letter of John Keats to John Taylor:

"Axioms in philosophy are not axioms until they are proved upon our pulses. We read fine things but never feel them to the full until we have gone the same steps as the Author."

BACKGROUND

As he did in the first stanza of "Ode on a Grecian Urn," the speaker in the fourth stanza is asking for information. Who are these people? What or where is the altar? Line 38 is a turning point in the poem because the speaker, for the first time, projects his imagination to a place not actually portrayed on the urn. He tries to create an image to answer his own question. In the fifth stanza, the speaker recoils from what his imagination has produced. The urn is no longer a source of feeling and meaning; it is now covered with "marble men and maidens," a "silent form." The speaker has been tempted in the course of his meditation to celebrate a pastoral world of idealized love and perfection, but he now recognizes that it is not the warm, sunny world he wanted. It is a world gone cold with the realization that the stoppage of time necessary for its perfection implies the permanence not only of love's anticipation but also of loneliness and desolation.

FOR DISCUSSION AND REFLECTION

➤ How does the emotional landscape alter in the fourth stanza? (Students should be able to point to the speaker's description of his imaginary "little town" that is "desolate" and where "streets for evermore / Will silent be.")

➤ What questions do you have about either particular images or the overall meaning of this poem? (Responses will vary.)

➤ Do you agree or disagree with Keats that "Beauty is truth, truth beauty"? (Encourage students to find examples from their own experience that support their point of view.)

Writing

QUICK ASSESS

Do students' responses:

✓ describe what they feel Keats is saying about time, art, beauty, and truth?

✓ include evidence from the poem as support?

Students are asked to explain what they think Keats is saying about time, art, beauty, and truth. Help them to formulate thesis statements that will then provide a focus for their quotes and direct references to the poem.

READING AND WRITING EXTENSIONS

➤ Have students read John Keats' "Ode to a Nightingale" and compare how it explores the human desire to escape the inevitable effects of living in a temporal world with how "Ode on a Grecian Urn" explores the theme.

➤ Ask students to imagine that they are a designer of contemporary American urns. Have them design a vase that depicts two different views of the world today. After they draw both sides of the vase, have students write a short, poetic description of each side, ending with Keats' final two lines.

Four Comparing Poems

Critical Reading

FOCUS

Similar to the figures on Keats' Grecian urn, in Maruyama's poem "The lion was, moment by moment, trying to kill; / The rhinoceros was, eternally, about to die."

BACKGROUND

After facing, and we hope meeting, the textual challenges posed by "Ode on a Grecian Urn," students are likely to be relieved to turn to Kaoru Maruyama's poem "A Rhinoceros and a Lion." This poem explores Keats' theme in modern free verse and contemporary language. Maruyama describes a scene from a painting of a lion attacking a rhinoceros: "Blood spouted up and, twisting his neck in agony, / The rhinoceros was looking at the sky."

FOR DISCUSSION AND REFLECTION

➤ How did you interpret the phrase "the landscape was silent"? (Many responses are possible, but they should include reference to the way a landscape in a painting never changes. The sky will be forever "blue and quiet." Students may also comment on how the landscape makes no judgment on what occurs between the animals. This is "An accidental moment in a far country of jungles . . . .")

➤ What effect did Maruyama's use of free verse have on you as a reader? (Some students may discount this poem for its lack of technical prowess compared with the poems by Shelley and Keats that they have read in this unit. Others are likely to feel that the poem's simple and straightforward language communicates more directly to them.)

➤ How did reading this poem make you feel? (Answers will vary depending upon students' attitudes toward animals in the wild, as well as to the theme of the poem— the timelessness of art.)

Writing

QUICK ASSESS

Do students' responses:

✔ discuss what the two poems have in common?

✔ discuss how the two poems are different?

Students are asked to explain what "A Rhinoceros and a Lion" and "Ode on a Grecian Urn" have in common. It should help them a great deal to review what they wrote about the Keats poem in the previous lessons.

READING AND WRITING EXTENSIONS

➤ Ask students to bring in photographs from magazines depicting an animal or animals in a natural habitat. Back issues of *National Geographic* are ideal for this assignment. Have students use a photo as a starting point for a poem of their own about this moment that the camera captured.

➤ Read students T. S. Eliot's poem "The Hippopotamus" and discuss how Eliot has used the creature for his own purposes.

Five Exploration and Interpretation

C r i t i c a l   R e a d i n g

FOCUS

T. S. Eliot believed that poetry lies not in an unbridled expression of emotion but in an escape from emotion.

BACKGROUND

Four Quartets was T. S. Eliot's last major poem. It was written between 1935 and 1942. Eliot believed it to be his finest achievement. Students may need some help to discover that the poem deals with ideas of incarnation, the intersection of time and eternity, and the discovery of spiritual insight in sudden and unexpected moments of revelation. More personal than his previous poems, *Four Quartets* is exquisitely lyrical and musical in structure.

FOR DISCUSSION AND REFLECTION

➤ Do you think Eliot's line "The stillness, as a Chinese jar still / Moves perpetually in its stillness" is consciously making reference to John Keats' first line in "Ode on a Grecian Urn"? (It may be a surprise to students that poets would carry other writers' words so close to their hearts that they might make reference to them either consciously or unconsciously. The point of this question is simply to speculate upon how great literature continues to influence writers.)

➤ How did you interpret the line "The Word in the desert / Is most attacked by voices of temptation . . . ." (Students unfamiliar with the New Testament may need to be told the story of Jesus' temptation in the desert by the devil.)

➤ What strategies do you use as a reader to help you make sense of a challenging poem like this one? (Many responses should be encouraged, including rereading. Help students to see how much they can figure out for themselves when they use what makes sense in individual lines to build an understanding of the whole poem.)

W r i t i n g

QUICK ASSESS

Do students' responses:

✓ use Eliot's phrases in a found poem of their own?

✓ reflect on what they have learned about Eliot's poetry?

Students are asked to create a found poem from words and phrases from T. S. Eliot's "Burnt Norton" and then reflect on what they learned about Eliot's poem from the process of composing their poems. In order to facilitate the manipulation of individual lines, have students copy quotations that strike them onto strips of paper. They can then arrange the strips in many different combinations until they achieve the poetic effect they want. You may also want to suggest that they repeat a particularly luminous phrase more than once in their poem.

READING AND WRITING EXTENSIONS

➤ Read to students Eliot's poem "Spleen." Have the class discuss possible interpretations together.

➤ Ask students to write about a time when they remember feeling that the world was standing perfectly still for a moment or two. Have them describe how they responded to this stillness.

Unit Overview

In this unit, students have the opportunity to immerse themselves in the world and writings of V. S. Naipaul. By examining excerpts from two of his novels and selections from his nonfiction works, students will discover how Naipaul creates strong characters, highlights unusual details, draws upon his experience and travels, and describes his intentions in writing.

Literature Focus

	Lesson	Literature
1.	Creating Characters	from "Hat" from *Miguel Street* (Novel)
2.	Replaying the Newsreel	"Prelude: An Inheritance" from *A Way in the World: A Novel* (Novel)
3.	Finding a Place in the World	"Prelude: An Inheritance" from *A Way in the World: A Novel* (Novel)
4.	The Writer in the World	from the Author's Foreword to *Finding the Center* (Nonfiction)
5.	A Portrait of the Writer	from "A Prologue to an Autobiography" from *Finding the Center* (Nonfiction)

Reading Focus

1. To create believable characters, writers use details and descriptions to answer the question, "What makes this character distinct?"
2. Authors do more than report their observations. They often bring out incongruous or unusual details to make their descriptions vivid.
3. Understanding the author's background and beliefs helps readers understand the meaning and ideas behind a story.
4. To write realistically about experiences, writers must be able to express to the reader the significance of the events.
5. Knowing how a writer describes the act of writing can help you understand his or her intentions in writing.

Writing Focus

1. Use an indirect method to characterize a person.
2. Find realistic images in the text and comment on the unusual aspects of the situation or characters.
3. Agree or disagree with one of Naipaul's ideas.
4. Describe an incident that you now understand differently than when it first occurred.
5. Write a brief sketch of Naipaul for someone who has never read his work.

One Creating Characters

Critical Reading

FOCUS

Endowed with the gift of being able "to give a fantastic twist to some very ordinary thing," V. S. Naipaul's character Hat takes a great deal of pleasure in being alive.

BACKGROUND

In his introduction to *Miguel Street,* Laban Erapu wrote that the novel is "more than merely a collection of short stories inter-linked by a common narrator. Although it is written in the form of individual character sketches, the setting gives unity and complexity to the community life that the book portrays. *Miguel Street* is essentially a memoir of childhood, recalled in exile with all the nostalgia and feeling of alienation that this is likely to arouse. The memories are characterized not so much by events as by the individuals through whom the child's waking consciousness comprehends and reconstructs his past."

FOR DISCUSSION AND REFLECTION

➤ The narrator tells us that Hat "was a bit like his dog." What did you infer he meant by this? (As students respond with generalizations, have them cite lines from the text to support their assumptions. Students should go beyond simply saying that Hat, like the dog, has a sense of humor. Both were also extremely resourceful and clever.)

➤ What does the example of the beautiful biting birds tell you about Hat? (Many responses are possible, but students should point to the suggestion that there is a dangerous side to Hat as well: "The macaws and the parrots looked like angry and quarrelsome old women and they attacked anybody.")

➤ Based upon this short excerpt, how would you characterize the narrator's relationship with Hat? (The young narrator seems to look up to Hat for his ingenuity. He also admires the natural joy Hat takes in just being alive: "He did nothing new or spectacular—in fact, he did practically the same things every day—but he always enjoyed what he did.")

Writing

QUICK ASSESS

Do students' descriptions:

✓ characterize a person through his or her possessions or habits?

✓ allow readers to infer key aspects of their character's personality?

Students are asked to write about someone they know, using his or her possessions and habits rather than direct description. Before they begin to write, have students talk in pairs about how their characters can be defined by an object or habit. This activity will help students to determine if they have enough material for their character sketches.

READING AND WRITING EXTENSIONS

➤ Have students read another character vignette from *Miguel Street*—for example, "B. Wordsworth"—which is about a mysterious self-styled poet who comes and goes like a figment of the imagination.

➤ Ask students to describe their mental picture of the narrator of *Miguel Street* using details from the story "Hat" to flesh out their assumptions.

Two Replaying the Newsreel

Critical Reading

FOCUS

From Salman Rushdie's essay, "Imaginary Homelands":

"Indian writers in these islands are capable of writing from a kind of double perspective: because they, we, are at one and the same time insiders and outsiders in this society."

BACKGROUND
Descended from Indians who had immigrated to Trinidad as indentured servants, V. S. Naipaul left Trinidad to attend Oxford University in 1950. He subsequently settled in England. His earliest books are ironic and satirical accounts of life in the Caribbean. Naipaul's later novels continued to examine the disintegration and the personal and collective alienation typical of postcolonial nations. V. S. Naipaul's writings express the ambivalence of exile, a feature of his own experience as an Indian in the West Indies, a West Indian in England, and a nomadic intellectual in the postcolonial world. *A Way in the World: A Novel* is about a writer coming to terms with his own nature.

FOR DISCUSSION AND REFLECTION
➤ Why do you think the people on the streets appear "darker than I remembered . . . ." to the narrator? (Students are likely to respond that since Naipaul lived in England among fair-skinned people for many years, he may be recalling the experience of returning to the Caribbean and finding its inhabitants "darker" by comparison not with their former selves, but with his more recent experience of people on the streets of London.)

➤ What can you infer from the narrator's comment that this story of Leonard Side came to him during a time of "fever"? (Many responses are possible, but students will probably want to discuss how, during his return visits to the island of St. James, the narrator often feels he is in a "half-dream, knowing and not knowing." It is during such times that he can come to new understandings about himself and his own nature.)

➤ How did the juxtaposition of the same fingers prodding a dead body and slipping little treats into women's mouths affect you as a reader? (Students are likely to share the teacher's distaste for Leonard Side, though, like her, also find it difficult to fault the man.)

Writing

QUICK ASSESS
Do students' lists:

✔ focus on five realistic images in the text?

✔ identify three incongruous details of the situation or characters?

Students are asked to find five realistic images in the text and then list unusual aspects of the situation. Remind students that most of our assumptions about what is strange versus what is ordinary are culturally based.

READING AND WRITING EXTENSIONS
➤ Have students read Salman Rushdie's essay "Imaginary Homelands" and discuss the creative dilemma faced by writers who cross cultures.

➤ Ask students to write a character sketch of a person in the news or media whose ideas or actions they find unethical or repulsive.

Three Finding a Place in the World

Critical Reading

FOCUS

Naipaul's narrator wonders whether Leonard Side ever comes "to some understanding of his nature; or whether the thing that had frightened the teacher had, when the time of revelation came, also frightened Leonard Side."

BACKGROUND

A Way in the World: A Novel is a closely woven blend of history, character study, and autobiography. Naipaul's descriptions of Trinidad reflect a mind whose every experience seems to have been captured in amber. The theme that repeats throughout is the shifting nature of reality as it is refracted through those who shaped Trinidad's colonial history as well as those who fumble for identity in its aftermath.

FOR DISCUSSION AND REFLECTION

➣ What do the repeated references to Leonard Side's "hairy fingers" suggest to you about the teacher's attitude toward the man? (Students may point to how, though she knows he is a good man, she finds Leonard Side somehow distasteful: "The mixing of things upset me.")

➣ Why do you think Naipaul includes historical and geographic details about the island of St. James? (He is pointing out to the reader that although he can compile many facts about the place, the facts still do not explain "the mystery of Leonard Side's inheritance." Naipaul's narrator suggests that some traits we inherit are inexplicable and do not follow the rules of genetic or cultural determinism.)

➣ What does the narrator's attitude toward Leonard Side reveal about the narrator? (Many responses are possible, but they should focus on how his desire to understand Leonard Side is a way of coming to understand himself.)

Writing

QUICK ASSESS

Do students' responses:

✓ agree or disagree with Naipaul's last sentence?

✓ include examples from the text and their own experience as support?

Students are asked to write about Naipaul's last line, "Sometimes we can be strangers to ourselves." To help students reflect on this quotation, ask them to think of a time when they watched themselves do something that seemed out of character at the time. What caused them to behave out of character? How did they feel afterward?

READING AND WRITING EXTENSIONS

➣ Have students go back and reread Jamaica Kincaid's essay "On Seeing England for the First Time" (pages 156–61) and discuss how V. S. Naipaul has explored some of the same themes in "Prelude: An Inheritance."

➣ Encourage students to go to the library to research the history and geography of the place that they or their parents came from originally.

Four The Writer in the World

Critical Reading

FOCUS

V. S. Naipaul explains that travel "broadened my world view; it showed me a changing world and took me out of my own colonial shell …."

BACKGROUND

In the last chapter of *Miguel Street*, the narrator's departure from Miguel Street and Trinidad is hastened by a phase of dissipation. The wild life he plunges into is a form of escape, but it is only a limited escape for one whose natural inclination is to get away from the disappointing changelessnes of this place. The scholarship to go abroad and study is the real escape he needs. To the West Indian of Naipaul's generation, this was tantamount to emigration, and the narrator's description of his departure suggests this: "I left them all and walked briskly towards the aeroplane, not looking back. Looking only at my shadow before me, a dancing dwarf on the tarmac."

FOR DISCUSSION AND REFLECTION

➤ How did you interpret Naipaul's description of being "glamoured by the idea of the long journey"? (Answers will vary, but students should work through the connotations of the word *glamour*. He is attracted to the thought of travel, intrigued by its possibilities, excited by the chance of adventure.)

➤ What does Naipaul say he had to learn how to do in order to look at a place "in a way that would be of value to other people"? (Among possible responses are the ability to move among strangers, to stay ready for revelation, and to follow his instincts.)

➤ What do you look for when you travel? What do you hope to experience? (Not all students will have traveled or dreamed of traveling. Be sensitive to students who avoid this question.)

Writing

QUICK ASSESS

Do students' descriptions:

✔ focus on an incident that they now understand differently than when it first occurred?

✔ express the incident's significance?

Students are asked to describe an incident in their own lives that they understand now in a way that they didn't when they were living through it. In "Prelude: An Inheritance," Naipaul describes the way the world looked differently with and without glasses. Have students describe the lens they now use to view their incident.

READING AND WRITING EXTENSIONS

➤ Have students reread Derek Walcott's poem "The Virgins" (page 73) and discuss together the differences between the reasons these tourists travel and Naipaul's reasons.

➤ Bring in travel brochures and posters from the Caribbean islands and have students write about the disjuncture between these pictures of life in the islands and the images presented in the works of Naipaul, Kincaid, and Walcott.

Five  A Portrait of the Writer

C r i t i c a l   R e a d i n g

FOCUS

Knowing what an author thinks about his or her writing process enriches your understanding of a work.

BACKGROUND

All good writing is characterized by rhythm. It is not an artificial construct of the writer but rather a natural feature of speech. Remind students that all speech is rhythmic, though not necessarily effectively rhythmic. Poets recognized long ago that language could be arranged into patterns that would both captivate the ear and intensify the emotion or meaning to be expressed by way of emphasis. In "A Prologue to an Autobiography" from *Finding the Center*, V. S. Naipaul describes his experience of working with sentences that "set up a rhythm, a speed, which dictated all that was to follow."

FOR DISCUSSION AND REFLECTION

➤ The lines from *Miguel Street* that begin this excerpt from "A Prologue to an Autobiography" are the first sentences of the novel. Why do you think Naipaul used them to help explain how he crafts his work? (Naipaul allows readers to see for themselves how his sentences flow one from the other and create "the world of the street.")

➤ Read this short excerpt aloud to hear the rhythms of Naipaul's sentences. What effect do these have on you as a reader? (Students are likely to describe how different his rhythms are from those of other writers from different cultures and climes.)

➤ Based upon your reading of these excerpts, do you think Naipaul succeeds in recreating the world of the street in Trinidad? (Answers will vary based upon students' personal responses to Naipaul's style and subject matter.)

W r i t i n g

QUICK ASSESS

Do students' writings:

✓ describe Naipaul as a writer?

✓ introduce Naipaul to someone unfamiliar with his work?

Students are asked to write a sketch of V. S. Naipaul the writer. Before they begin, make a list on the board of all the character traits students can discern from the selections in these lessons.

READING AND WRITING EXTENSIONS

➤ Have students research V. S. Naipaul and share what they have found that might be useful to include in their sketches of the writer. (One resource is Paul Theroux's essay on his friendship with Naipaul in the August 8, 1998, issue of *The New Yorker*.)

➤ Ask students to collect interesting snippets of conversation that seem to have a particular rhythm. They may or may not choose to reveal the identity of the speakers when they read to the class what they have collected.

I n d e x

Teacher's Guide page numbers are in parentheses following pupil's edition page numbers.

SKILLS

allusion, 152 (TG 152)

annotating, 10 (TG 30),

argument, 172 (TG 105), 175 (TG 106)

biographical details, 18 (TG 34), 73 (TG 58), 88 (TG 66), 153 (TG 96), 199 (TG 119), 202 (TG 121)

characterization, 130 (TG 85), 146 (TG 93), 177 (TG 107), 200 (TG 120)

conflict, 26 (TG 37), 52 (TG 49)

connecting to experience, 12 (TG 31)

context, 152 (TG 96), 154 (TG 97), 159 (TG 99)

details, 55 (TG 50), 65 (TG 55)

figures of speech, 178 (TG 108)

genre, 43 (TG 45), 59 (TG 52), 104 (TG 73), 164 (TG 102), 179 (TG 109)

imagery, 15 (32), 16 (TG 33), 30 (TG 39), 102 (TG 72)

inferences, 118 (TG 79)

irony, 73 (TG 58)

language/word use, 16 (TG 33), 93 (TG 63), 139 (TG 89), 140 (TG 90), 142 (TG 91), 144 (TG 92), 179 (TG 109)

meter, 91 (TG 67)

modeling, 79 (TG 61), 81 (TG 62), 83 (TG 63)

ode, 81 (TG 62), 190 (TG 115)

opinion, 169 (TG 104)

perspective, 14 (TG 32), 71 (TG 32), 156 (TG 98)

point of view, 14 (TG 32), 57 (TG 51), 131 (TG 86), 164 (TG 102)

predictions, 114 (TG 78)

purpose, 123 (TG 82)

rhyme/rhythm, 77 (TG 60), 91 (TG 67), 105 (TG 73), 106 (TG 74)

satire, 58 (TG 51)

sources, 50 (TG 48)

setting, 43 (TG 45)

theme, 89 (TG 66), 119 (TG 80)

tone, 28 (TG 38), 185 (TG 112)

voice, 83 (TG 63)

WRITING

argument, 174 (TG 105)

book cover, 20 (TG 34)

chart, 16 (TG 33), 19 (TG 34), 27 (TG 37), 32 (TG 39), 56 (TG 50), 60 (TG 52), 85 (TG 64), 112 (TG 76), 118 (TG 79), 128 (TG 84), 167 (TG 103)

description, 64 (TG 54), 70 (TG 56), 74 (TG 58), 141 (TG 90), 176 (TG 106), 201 (TG 120), 214 (TG 124)

drawing, 17 (TG 33), 107 (TG 74), 194 (TG 117)

emulation, 84 (TG 63)

essay, 34 (TG 40)

glossary, 141 (TG 90)

letter, 153 (TG 96)

paragraph, 11 (TG 30), 37 (TG 42), 155 (TG 97)

personal narrative, 13 (TG 31), 95 (TG 68), 100 (TG 70), 129 (TG 84)

poem, 14 (TG 32), 72 (TG 57), 78 (TG 60), 80 (TG 61), 82 (TG 62), 86 (TG 64), 92 (TG 67), 110 (TG 75), 158 (TG 98), 162 (TG 100), 198 (TG 118)

scene/story, 42 (TG 44), 48 (TG 46), 138 (TG 88), 143 (TG 91), 150 (TG 94), 158 (TG 98), 191 (TG 115)

summary, 51 (TG 48), 77 (TG 60), 121 (TG 80), 184 (TG 111)

translation, 145 (TG 92)

web, 62 (TG 54), 91 (TG 67)

writing about fiction, 25 (TG 36), 29 (TG 38), 34 (TG 40), 37 (TG 42), 42 (TG 43), 46 (TG 45), 97 (TG 69), 117 (TG 78), 121 (TG 80), 133 (TG 86), 136 (TG 87), 148 (TG 93), 209 (TG 122)

writing about nonfiction, 51 (TG 48), 54 (TG 49), 58 (TG 51), 60 (TG 52), 67 (TG 55), 112 (TG 76), 124 (TG 82), 161 (TG 99), 166 (TG 102), 171 (TG 104), 205 (TG 121), 213 (TG 124)

writing about poetry, 11 (TG 30), 13 (TG 31), 15 (TG 32), 17 (TG 33), 82 (TG 62), 90 (TG 66), 103 (TG 72), 108 (TG 74), 155 (TG 97), 178 (TG 108), 181 (TG 109), 183 (TG 110), 184 (TG 111), 186 (TG 112), 189 (TG 114), 193 (TG 116), 195 (TG 117), 197 (TG 118)

L e s s o n   T i t l e   I n d e x

Literature Index